DANCING
THROUGH
THE
LABYRINTH

MITCHELL L.J. POCO

For Jake.

CONTENTS

PREFACE

The following is something like a love child between devotion to the English language and a restless itch for philosophical clarity. I claim no formal academic instruction in either beyond the rudiments presented in secondary school — most of this work was drafted living across the United States on the back of a motorcycle, careening from the tail end of a psychedelic mishap and an abruptly terminated military career. Though the space beyond what winding corridors lie herein might grace your back with happy pleas for a safe return — understand surprise will be unwarranted if the domain encountered upon the final closure of this tome is not quite so familiar as the one left behind. Reading this backward will not be helpful in reversing that.

Travel well.

1

DISSOLUTION, TRANSMUTING CHAOS

E very being exists in a twofold situation; half its quality is potential — what lies past the horizon, underground, and beneath the point sunlight pierces; the other is immediate — what lies prior to the horizon, on the surface, and is clearly perceptible in the sunlight's illumination. With every movement, the boundaries defining the familiar and unfamiliar domains are proportionately adjusted in relation to one's locus of perception. If understanding expands, so too does the portion of unexplored territory in contact with its surface area. Should one explore, traded is the understanding attained in their headlights' illumination, for what's abandoned beyond the reach of their taillights.

How is the quality of being to be assessed, then, when each is not only bound by the inherently limited fragment of their own understanding, but also perceptually isolated from those which shape the template for anyone else's progress? Attempting to derive usable information via comparison is always in deliberate ignorance to the incongruence between the milieu wherein another's development occurs, and one's own. That being said, the continual reference of others' expressed perspectives is unavoidably the means by which one develops their own approach — which is fitting, because the incompleteness characterizing that partial relation isn't just a reflection of the aforementioned incompleteness endemic to understanding itself, but to everything else, as well; logs composing a cabin wall rely on each other, but never occupy precisely the same space; the strokes of an engine each occupy precisely the same space, but accomplish inverse chemical processes; the notes of a song are organized in a balance of variation and repetition, etc. If such were not the case, the contents of space-time would be undifferentiated — a difficult conception given the painful self-evidence that a cabin wall cannot possess an infinitude of separate logs, or merely one log; energy cannot be harvested from a four-stroke engine whose pistons only suck, squeeze, bang, or blow, and the chords emitted from a piano upon which a cat chases its tail do not a song make, just as John Cage's 4'33"...

Quantifying the grace an organism possesses in tacking through the chaotic winds of the universe isn't at all a straightforward task, for essentially the same reason that any fish judged for its tree-climbing capacity is incompetent compared to a monkey. No fixed standard exists in the totality (or lack thereof) of the universe. Vast strata of competence are a non-negotiable environmental precondition for creatures to belong to niches wherein they can flourish — niches being unexploited vacuums whose boundaries are drawn by the unique capacities of other creatures.

Given this, any yardstick intended to measure adaptability would fall appallingly short of being useful in the hands of the most seasoned wildlife biologist — and be instantly recognizable as a bastardization of matter itself as a thing meant for use in the human sphere, where success only begins to be defined light-years past the minimum threshold of survival, and is interpretable in as many ways as there are people. Still though, the inclination to conceive a means of being which would tie as many loose ends as possible, overcome the necessity for adaptation as such, and banish insofar as it's possible the notion of insecurity itself — is the alchemical urge to generate the Philosopher's Stone, the Christian longing for salvation, the scientific drive to discover what lay at the bottom of physics, etc. Little between nobility or foolishness do these pursuits typically call to mind, as their attainment would be in direct contravention to the structure of life itself — the ethereal allure they possess the very catalysts for progress. Humans are intrinsically averse to stagnance. This said — the impossibility of attaining true invulnerability, when regarded as a thing binding one's life to the punchline of some terrible cosmic joke, is disdainfully misrepresented. The unreachable goals striven toward by Earth's various cultures are taken seriously because what keeps a human in motion is the unwavering presence of two inverse characteristics, just as a coin spins on the edge of two indispensable sides — they are the following: The expectation of closure (somewhat ironically ill-defined owing to the experiential incommunicability of death, which epitomizes closure), and an insistence on pushing past perceptible boundaries.

On a superficial level — it's outright contradictory to express gratitude for vulnerability against which no defense can be mustered, especially considering the array of nightmares it's liable to manifest as: cancer, rape, fratricide, harlequin ichthyosis — just to name a bundle. The only thanks to give such a force is for what growth it might enable. This, however, is effectively no different from the subset of thanks given to anything regarded as positively and obviously good in the world. The distinction between positive and negative stimuli is essentially borne from the insistence that each phenomenological ripple be cordoned off from every other in accordance with a conveniently cognized schedule. As an elementary illustration: the minimum standard of descriptive fidelity isn't as demanding in the analysis of things perceived to be so variable that their changeability is implied in their assessment — e.g., to describe a traffic light as green is not a controversial assessment, because its lighted hue is both focal and taken for granted to differ over brief periods, with the inverse being the case for something like a mountain, which for all intents and purposes is a static fixture despite its relative size, lifetime, and thus total change undergone, being vastly greater. For anything relating to oneself, whether a judgment about one's own nature, or regarding the nature of something having affected oneself — the dubious continuity of the perspective generating the assessment precludes the faithful implication of changeability *or* persistence, meaning it's not only constantly uncertain to what degree accuracy is intended to be conveyed in such instances, but to what degree it is, intentions aside. Drawing conclusions related to the self is like laying bets intended for Texas hold 'em, with the possibility that the game could change to blackjack, or cornhole, or anything else, at any moment.

For something comparably simple as far as raw complexity is concerned, the combustion engine is a thing which, for the purposes allotted it, is perfectly justified in its existence the moment it's fitted with wheels, a frame, and a few hundred other bits of hard and soft-ware, at which point it's a car or a train — unmistakable in its utility, and cut slack where it's criticized on account of its role as an integral feature of the greater socioeconomic landscape. Humans and their trifles are not afforded such a comfortable pouch wherein from each angle assurance exists that everything is grand just 'long as so many wheels keep turning. They exist at the bleeding edge of creation, and in return for their entitlement to sculpt new vistas of reality, forfeit is the luxury to follow trodden tracks on their quest through what would, to an animal of lesser cognitive capacity, be the mundane plane; let alone en route to encounter the genuine upper limits of their potential. The cradle made from "that which is obvious" does not exist for something as absurd as a human being. On the purely physical level — problems akin to the necessity for an oil change arise, and may be remedied with straightforward means. The vast sum of issues, however, whose presence in people's minds bets are safe to place regarding which hold the most weight — are the type alike in nature to the seeds people sow cultivating the spectacle that is their lives. I.e., seeds containing enormous, self-replicating futures of boundless possibility, whose edges even in infancy would be impossible to point at with a stick because of their unretractable and compounding enmeshment with every conceivable fold of local (and in due time far-reaching) reality; things whose chemical equivalents would conjure ineffable quantities of dismay if spilled in a laboratory.

The human animal's dignity, thankfully, is preserved as a token of their dilemma's undiscardable awkwardness, and so in some sense the means to live effectively may be simplified to the act of pressing on an accelerator — that what disconcerting details would otherwise leer into the cockpit of carnal navigation might be obscured. The tricky bit rears its head when attempting to distinguish which road to travel will be preferable in retrospect before starting off on one. Supposing the absence of regret tops one's list of priorities, the sheer time investment of a serious cost-benefit analysis surrounding which decisions to make would have the staunchest logistician throwing as much caution into as much wind as humanly possible as their final days encroached — their best years spent furtively manning a weigh-station for pros and cons.

It may not be possible to delineate from individual to individual which types of actions each should take to properly fill even a *brief* space of time. It appears that any point of reference, such as the life of one's friend or parent, can just as arbitrarily incite revulsion as stir inspiration — completely independent of things like greater cultural standing or other generic markers denoting who qualifies as role-model material. The skills and values a society aspires to emulate are as directly representative of individual aspirations as the average height of a population is of any specific member (which, for the sake of elucidation, could mean not at all). It sounds like it makes sense that the masses would fall on a bell curve between "unacceptable" and "excelling," but when the breadth of each person's predilections are nigh-guaranteed to plot across the whole expanse measuring taboo to saintly given the frequency of polar inversion examples of each experience over the course of millennia, due to the binary nature of human morality combined with cognitive crystallization effectively randomizing which qualities persist as "virtuous" to the most recent members of even something with as little variability as a single family lineage (compared to the culture, or world, at large) — the specific tendencies sat along the x-axis of such a curve may as well be pitched into a running jet turbine and concatenated from left to right where they fall. Normally, the chaotic undercarriage of societal preference, if encountered, traumatizes on first contact — evoking a kind of Hail Mary approach at organizing a game plan for moving forward which involves blindly casting stigma in the direction of anything remotely resembling one's personal conception of moral ambiguity, and a thick layering of emotional concrete on whichever habits have offered the most functional personal security from birth to the present.

Amusingly enough, the *dearth* of precision involved in conveying meaning with language, even when correctly executed according to the most crystalline body of its evolving ruleset (a rarity unto itself; over half of Americans read below a sixth-grade level), is arguably the reason culture functions at all. The presence of so many basic contradictions and misunderstandings lurking about virtually all discourse fertilizes an ecosystem where the primary substrate from which the many miracles of society emerge is composed of comfortable silence, meaningless banter, and the simple absence of bodily threat.

There are no truly reliable indicators which would reveal the presence of any viscerally repulsive or irresistibly attractive perspectives in anyone. Even far past the point of familiar conversation, the amount of definitional rectification to be made at every turn of phrase in order to sort out how someone else's nervous system is reacting in response to one's words — each with their own deep, subconscious, paradigm-entangled roots, counts very easily as potentially years of work at the pace the average person is comfortable doing that sort of thing.

Evidently, the glue in large part holding things together is the peace made with the enormous lack of understanding buffering the space between it all. Suppose three people find themselves sitting together, obligated to discuss the best way to handle a problem which is sufficiently complex that as of yet experts in the field pertaining to it haven't arrived at a consensus regarding its solution. Each set of experts views the others as incurably stupid (straining the meaning of the term "expert"), and two of the three interlocutors abides by opposing ends of the argument. The third is content to withhold themselves from identifying with a position, but sees in each faults and merits alike, as well as the portion of time it would take to straighten out why from behind each bulwark the other would appear so unforgivable from an emotional perspective, to the end of establishing empathy between them. The only shot at facilitating a dialogue uniting those holding the keys to a working solution is in leveraging whatever common ground can be revealed by that neutral entity's ability to preserve investigative integrity following the inquiry,

"Who knows?"

Otherwise, like the contents of a pinless grenade, the opinionated parties would rapidly tear apart from one another. This type of balance is extrapolatable to any scale — from within the individual to the planet at large. The key point isn't so much that a violent fission event would occur if what's not understood fails to be respected as such in a given scenario (not that that's beyond the realm of possibility), but that to what degree it's written off or chocked up will be that to which the margin of error's maximum breadth is trimmed once a solution is brought to bear.

The other matter perpetually thrown into disarray by the presence of the unknown is that of persistence. The instant a course of action is selected, prior to the first twitch indicating a start in its direction — an appalling amount of information, warping and shifting, concealing and disguising the true nature of the relevant objective, comes to flood the interpretive matrix one maps across reality. With the amount of apprehendable data at any person's disposal, and subsequently the colossal amount of data that's impossible to account for, one may feel as an ancient Earthling possessed of preposterous longevity, moving slowly so as to be operating on a scale of millions of years — tasking themselves to reach a point on the far side of Pangaea, with the continents splitting and drifting underfoot all the while. It's debatable whether the "point" continues to exist if the context in which it's originally defined becomes wholly unrecognizable.

If one considers a goal they have for themselves, then stands in place and selects an arbitrary point some forty meters in the distance, reasoning as though it truly represents their destination, and walks toward it — the number of reasons not to go on with it, as to why it's stupid, why other people might suppose it's weird, or out of character, or a waste of time, and that simply make the endeavor maddeningly uncomfortable, arise in droves. For perspective — suppose the actual goal, at a glance, could be feasibly attained on the order of three month's time; assuming one walks forty meters in a minute, to accurately anticipate the gross quantity of minute-to-minute stress associated with its accomplishment, multiply the laundry list of mentally unsettling variables something approximating one-hundred-thirty thousand times, to say nothing of the potential for physical difficulty. Selecting a direction to head in can be deceptively simple for a vanishingly brief period of time, because it seems as though the goal itself is subject to destruction on account of everything around it that's in flux.

Any goal's fixedness, however, has a shifting primary dependence between they who set it, and all the things surrounding it. For some, the execution of every worldly activity is conditionally predicated on the absence of precipitation, while for others, the apotheosis of their favorite passtime is only reached with the grace of a potentially lethal tsunami. The degree of chaos a person is capable of and willing to embrace is equivalent to the amount of slack they've tucked close in a spool as they pull themselves toward the manifestation of their intent, with, conversely, the lack thereof equal to the amount being unmanageably flung about in the wind. In other words — chaos is functionally nothing more than as-of-yet employed leverage. Death itself isn't even beyond the human capacity for transforming obstacles into stepping stones; consider the myriad legends who're immortalized because their demise catalyzed a supernova of popularity, or the (literally and figuratively) biblical force of martyrdom.

A given path's complexity isn't intrinsically greater or lesser than another's, or even than the rotunda wherein their entrances converge. Tentatively stepping half-assedly in and out of their thresholds, fretting at a fork down the road beyond one, or seizing at the thought that any of them if granted commitment would permanently tint one's personal history thereafter — all stand as equals in their potential to yield any more than barren gaps of time. An individual's efficacy in characterizing potential decisions as superfluous or indispensable relative to their most overarching conceivable objective is what determines the complexity of their endeavor. It's likely that that parent objective will escape articulation, or appear to change over time, because it can only present itself as a series of milestones — humans being temporally limited. Similar to how at any time in a song's composition, the main priority is to play the next note, even though the total value exists in every note played from start to finish — because from below the fourth-dimension there's no other way to approach the endeavor.

If one attempts to hold every turn they've mapped ahead in their head as they proceed, the point is missed, because though the graceful compilation of maneuvers does warrant celebration — to competently append each to the last requires undivided attention. In the execution of anything original, a calling in some general direction is all that's necessary. If the presently prescribed heading is attended with discipline and focus, the eddies of seemingly unmanageable chaotic novelty that arise become clear as especially important to the greater structure of the enterprise — and the equivalence between upheavals in one's personal pursuits as they heed their call, to the peculiarly organized explosion of a flower from its drab stalks, is revealed.

Perhaps the strangest thing about successful adaptation is that there is in fact a path to walk — but like a sentence that can only be jarringly interrupted if one attempts to affix the final clause preemptively, and like a hand-woven sari which will never be crafted precisely as such ever again, it cuts miraculously through untrammeled woods, straight to its destination. As it goes, the sentiments binarily accosting the reality of original execution — that it's illusory, and that everything is totally original, both miss the mark the same way a person yanking on a locked door and one walking past it both ultimately fail to traverse its threshold. On one hand, no two circumstances are replicable, and on the other, the only means to advance is from some point existing in relation to all others. Why, despite the insane variance produced by such a mechanic, are the categories of effect separate from "neutral," those synonymous with improvement, and those synonymous with degradation? How is it that such instinctual admiration and aversion can persist in an existence where everything is so inextricably interwoven?

One of the oddest things humans do to provoke these questions is divorce themselves and their categorically destructive behavior from a majority subset of worldly processes they've dubbed "nature." This seems, thoroughly, to be a culturally sanctioned ploy designed to shirk responsibility for an array of activities by passively facilitating woeful sentiments toward that which humanity exploits — but little more. The obligation to show the rest of the non-human world attention without blindly razing it only tastes synthetic and unactionable because a boundary has been conceptually imposed which divides the full swath of human intent from a system of ethics potentially orders of magnitude broader and deeper than it's currently permitted to be. It isn't apparent that it demands less energy to identify a sector of human qualities inherently undesirable — voluntarily engaging in a perpetually losing battle, than it is to abandon the false partition between humans and nature, embracing the full extent of the damage done as a thing not only voluntarily inflicted, but voluntarily *self*-inflicted.

The word "nature" and the word "everything" should be synonymous insofar as the latter isn't being used to describe the enclosed contents of any conceptual container (the former, in accordance, will henceforth be used with it interchangeably). Nature, to date, is a scapegoat of a phrase which makes it seem like an insurmountable waste of time to approach the actualities of human effect with anything more sincere or detailed than a sigh accompanied by vague and ultimately ignorable sensations of dismay. It's a hall-pass for ignorance, because "everything" is too big and scary for anyone to be expected to sort through. People deceive themselves into thinking interfacing with everything isn't what they're doing when they do anything — attempting to don blinkers assuming the net stress they're ingesting is somehow less than they would otherwise.

The human mind will narrate any space at any level of magnification with the full force of one thousand filled opera houses in terms of emotional, intellectual, and physical salience — the extra energy spent fearfully trimming off what gets perceived isn't even thrown in the furnace in exchange for a personal or societal Band-Aid, the integrity of human perception rejects any such thing as a rule. That energy gets scrapped in exchange for *nothing*. Fear, instead of acting as the insurmountable barrier corralling most into their various ruts, takes on a sort of comedic absurdity when it's accepted to be wholly inescapable. The fear of death and the fear of stigmatization for wearing a certain outfit can register as physiologically identical; everyone's running on the same wetware. Understanding this doesn't make the phenomenon any less potent, but regarded as a basic function which can be observed instead of avoided each time it arises, it's infinitely more manageable. Its inverse, feelings of overwhelming, manic infallibility — hold the potential to be even more crippling than mismanaged fear. The kind of directionless joy promised in heaven isn't scarce on Earth just for the sake of a taunt; in virtually every manifestation the thing is a disabling poison which facilitates nothing but decay and the expedited arrival of death. Particularly, the North American infatuation with instant gratification and the antagonization of hardship in and of itself indicates a grievously deleterious misunderstanding of what amount each is healthily optimal, and, indeed, appreciable in.

It's readily observable that what is sweet, colorful, olfactorily pleasant, predatorily robust, and generally a wellspring whereto attention gravitates — is disproportionately infrequent in its emergence compared to everything else. This is so the case that the word "rare" incites feelings of awe when its use is in earnest. Despite it blatantly being clear to the degree that in all instances where a brief glimmer of iridescence in the otherwise uniform sea of phenomena produces an instinctually visceral sense of appreciation, very frequently all that's perceived upon its departure is a childish, fretful longing for its immediate return. There is such a pervasive myopia with respect to the fact that the total area of a tree's apples being quantitatively minuscule compared to that of the rest of the tree, is the only reason apples are so many thousands of times sweeter than wood — that the illustration seemingly repeats itself in the ratio of those capable of appreciating the fact to the vast swath who walk through life's inconceivably lush gardens tearful for how much dirt there is.

Never among those who fill this world's voids with light as stars in the skies at night reside sentiments bemoaning the incredulity of those long, dark stretches. Flicker — burning for what duration they're embraced; embrace them as a matter of course — dine upon the abyss itself.

Occasional berries are meant to justify their own pursuit, not to rend one's sanity as they're maniacally clawed after and hoarded. The travesty of such behavior is it makes one incapable of tasting a bounty in its full force, just as untrimmed fruits sap the flavor of the rest. Most notably, such counterproductive tendencies arise when the labor of generations past is used as a means to ameliorate a developing person's discontentment without forethought. The habit of orienting oneself to reward, cordoning off the entire domain of prerequisite striving as one littered with evils necessary only insofar as they can't be detoured around and ignored — is to the human spirit as a farmer who lays and dreams of their harvest instead of engaging with the soil, is to their crop. Life in all its forms has no lack of resilience at its disposal — too frequently its use is cast aside in favor of anxious but "safely" sequestered dwelling, as though the practice could bring anything aside from perpetually unmet expectation into being.

Like bait cast into the sea without a line attaching it to the fisher are wishes imposed on the world without the requisite willingness to personally fulfill them. So divorced can one's vision for the future become from any immediate intent by behaving as such for long enough — that the neglected hope, forcing itself to be expressed, leaks from the orifices as a condemnable, fermented mass; the putrid, rotting spectacle wiped away apathetically by souls apparently punishing themselves with its continued presence merely for shame of not having attended it earlier.

2

ESTIMATION AND EXECUTION

The capacity to deal with a given problem is often handicapped by a refusal to limit one's spectrum of concern to the outer borders of present manageability. This misstep is fatal not only because it results in catastrophic energy loss (anxiety associated with parts of the garden one cannot yet reach serves no purpose, and is therefore parasitic) — but because those needlessly attended limits grow in relation with one's progress, and so the expectation that progress will shrink them can hurl one into the bowels of a Sisyphean nightmare. It should be noted, though, that if one cannot establish some means to perceive Sisyphean existence rewarding, or at least muster the will to proceed in spite of it, the remaining options are delusion or suicide.

There is value in stretching the depth of perception as far as possible, because it will ensure one's action contains the maximal expression of personal ability, but it should be done ritualistically — as a means to that end. If it's done in nihilistic fits as a means to justify prolonged inaction preceded by any modicum of headway, one may as well shank their own eyes in expectation of an ophthalmologist appointment, or dip their genitals in a vat of acid prior to sex; life becomes little more than a parade of self-inflicted torture.

To move with grace, the understated ease cultivated from maintaining a steady forward orientation in the face of potentially insurmountable odds is of critical necessity. That capacity is developed through the practice of sitting in fear without distraction. On a given path, brief moments of highly-concentrated discomfort are what invoke the throwing-in of the towel. By using prolonged discomfort opportunistically, the stopping-power of those moments can be drastically dampened — just as the thousands of rounds put downrange in military training are in anticipation of one half-second where fractional percentages of speed and accuracy spell the difference between success and failure.

One cannot expect themselves to engage with the high-stress demands intermittently scattered before them by assuming they take themselves seriously enough that no issue will present itself — just as one declaring

"Bro, I got this," as a substitute for regularly working out, will inevitably collapse beneath what may have otherwise been reasonably managed weight, with consistent practice. Honing oneself as such may feel like pointless toil in preparation for endless strife, but a significant difference between training and application, if done correctly, is that the latter is the easier of the two, and not just because the obstacles should be fewer and further between than in the conditions imposed upon oneself. The energy made available when playing for real stakes is proportional to the increase in risk, not dissimilar to the maneuverability gained when one removes training wheels from a bicycle. To those who are cautious, with a regular vigilance in regard to their own shortcomings, will that energy present itself as a true boon — for it's possible to overestimate what leeway it grants. Conversely, those types reap its benefits infrequently compared to those enthusiastic to take advantage of it, because they doubt themselves sufficiently competent to chance stepping into domains that aren't simulatory quite as often.

In the midst of pursuit, those two characters' tendencies as they lose traction tend to reflect their respective approaches. The passive, calculating type will retreat into a position where they can give themselves perspective on the problem at hand from a higher elevation — wary of reentering struggle until at least the intimation of some scheme for proceeding has made itself known. The headstrong variety becomes unhinged and chaotic — seeking triumph in a final crusade of force.

Contrary precepts are touted in respect to the optimal method for overcoming predicaments generally, and are reflected in the attitudes of the aforementioned classes — distillable, essentially, into offense and defense. To capitalize on what strengths one already possesses (offense), and to focus on the remediation of one's weaknesses (defense). The only way, as in anything, to accurately discern the necessary of the two approaches, is to evaluate the circumstances wherein their prioritization is being called into question, since a complete lack of either renders one impotent.

Curiously, though, in theory — a perfect offense or defense compensates for the absence of its opposite, the descriptor "perfect" denoting invulnerability. Differentiation between the two collapses in this case, because it would mean "an offense so strong, it functions as a defense," and vice versa. This may paint the picture of why it's as though there are separate camps in approaching life from these two perspectives — each striving to manifest a version of their method so completely that it would cancel out the necessity of implementing the other.

This is a wasteful, graceless, childish way to delegate resources. The optimal way is to ascertain which aspect, if attended to, would suit the current predicament with minimal energy expenditure, just as the puck's position relative to the lines dividing the ice in a hockey game determine which portion of the team is activated, while the other assumes what's more or less a position of support. Attending strengths and weaknesses is functionally no different from attending the accelerator and the brakes, respectively.

The best relationship between these two things is the kind which conceals the functions of both — when the pushing and pulling poles of a situation are in such smooth accordance that the transfer of energy from one to the other, and subsequently, the explicit purpose of either, is swept away from perception on account of the density and rapidity with which fluid sophistication is made manifest. The relationship between the two aspects becomes the pinnacle of both — resulting in an entirely new phenomenon, independent of either.

Personal elevation, hockey, racing, and every system imaginable depends on the cooperation between independent substructures. An interesting facet of their interplay is that each is easily overlooked while the system is "running" or "going on," with those constituents becoming distinguishable in a snapshot, or series thereof, if they occupy separate spaces, or are actuated in separate intervals, respectively. Demonstrated by this fact is an element of particular importance pertaining to independence and cooperation — which is that the distance between them is crossed based on nothing more than the presently demarcated context.

Since either is never truly secondary to the other — nature existing on the basis of cooperating units which could not cooperate if they themselves weren't markedly unique in some respect — the fundamental distinction between disintegration and integration is hardly cogent in the final analysis, despite the force with which it may present itself in a given circumstance. It sounds nuts, because it sort of throws any coherent implications into the blender; the stability of a supposition relies on the hard line before which things are one way, and beyond which things are another.

It isn't quite that those dichotomies are false, but they always serve ends aimed at to the exclusion of possible outcomes which inextricably define them — meaning to involve with them constitutes the perpetuation of exactly as much of what they're leveraged to avoid as what one hopes they'll facilitate. To make a friend is to make their enemies one's own, to register to vote is to shoulder the resultant political turbulence, to act in favor of one's conception of good is to nurture the possibility of an equal opposite reality of evil.

With the basic configuration being "point-and-shoot," and the knowledge that every target will cast its shadow, the only matter one can sanely concern themselves with is what distance to place it — because how far into the future one intends to focus their efforts will necessitate taking potentially counterproductive actions relative to another time frame. As far as the most digestible temporal hazards, living as though every moment is one's last is liable to make for an appalling mess over time — and likely even shorten one's lifespan, whereas plotting far into the future in a bid to carve one's legend into the annals of history calls for absurd amounts of work, a potentially thankless existence for the duration, and an absolutely goofy exit scene if death comes knocking before the seed for the grand plan has been adequately cultivated. It's just as reasonable to weigh every second as an amazing privilege, as it is to fight and toil to create something that blows some other high achievement out of the water, as it is to work just enough to kick it on the weekends. One thing that's certain is that the attention given to a certain way of being will absolutely contribute to its manifestation, and if it's absorbed in things one has distaste for because they're unaware to what degree their future should or could be schemed out, their life will be hijacked like a Cordyceps-infected ant corpse — working mindlessly on behalf of some ungraspable force.

The endeavor, whatever it is, and whether anyone knows what it is, is most definitely underway. There are blind spots that cannot be accounted for without creating more, and there are troves of information which could make the most perilous journeys worth every step. It's terrifying and glorious that the simple act of facing a particular direction will bring its horizon's contents into one's grasp given enough time. The world is like a thing every creature is married to the instant they're born, the vow sealed and the enterprise carried out until the partition of death comes crashing down, for better or for worse, whatever it means. To scream until blood leaks from one's lips or to laugh in a genuine fit of hysterics or to eat figs or to live in a cave or to sing opera or to feed millions or to avenge ferrets or to walk only east or to do a flip — are all on the table like Thanksgiving dinner laid out by a senile jester on two-thousand mics of salvia who's been given permission by some insane god to serve whatever they please. It's a vast scene, and anything goes. It's just as feasible to establish security that lasts ten-thousand years as it is to slip and nuke every inhabited inch of Earth.

With everyone vying for their own energies and patterns to permeate the zeitgeist — whether one succeeds in doing as little as organizing their private lives in a specific manner is hugely predicated on how much information they'll manage to consciously discard (not preemptively avoid perceiving). The spectrum of human intent colors the surface of consensus reality so completely that hesitation in imposing one's own boundaries will turn their energy into fertilizer for whatever forces in the vicinity hold the highest bid to exploit it — and quicker than most are able to figure what their standards even vaguely ought to resemble. The metaphor of "carving oneself" into what one desires isn't used in common discourse for no reason — humans resemble bonsai in that their beauty emerges in terms of how many latent potential outcomes they've sacrificed for the sake of their designs. For one's constituent parts to cooperate to the end of producing a phenomenal individual, clutter in the forms of malfunctioning relationships, addictions, physical excess, compartmentalized emotions, and the like — need to be mercilessly composted. People seem to shy from this on account of it being "too painful," but endure all flavors of counterproductive and unnecessary suffering as the trade-off for leaving them in place.

The primary opposing walls in the arena of actualization unwittingly clung to, are characterized by shameless pleas for respite among hordes who face the same daunting objective of creating some dignified, worthwhile version of themselves — and blank glares propounding dumbfounded denial that anyone would ever be expected to manage a problem as complex as the one they face. The only explanation for either attitude, both of which indefinitely bar any type of growth, boils down to fear. It's an odd thing to reference as of gravity here, because it's eliminated by reining-in one's capacity to project into the future — but for the exact purpose of facilitating the future's emergence in a way that's preferable. To reasonably justify the discardment of fear, traversal to the centermost point of the arena needs to be clearly illustrated as it unfolds from each end.

On the hand whereby difficulty is shied-away from, it's imperative to possess some spirit of "that which can overcome obstacles," and clarify to oneself that surrender to whatever circumstances one struggles against, no matter how frequently and with what force they strike, is to forfeit a very real war whose culmination will inscribe the immutable score of one's existence vs. The World. On the hand whereby complexity is shied-away from, faith in one's ability to unequivocally foster a path forward which will stand righteously through the passage of time is a crucial asset, because no external justification will arrive on a silver platter from the heavens; credence in it cannot be bestowed from anywhere external to oneself.

As the center is approached, the object against which fear proves useful transforms into what necessitates the implementation of anger as a means to push through — until eventually that too can be discarded, and one can dedicate their focus to ensuring calm, secure maintenance of a mental and physical centrality from which they're exalted. The whole process is comparable to that of relinquishing victim-hood, declaring war, annexing territory, and cultivating something new and wonderful (until that dies and the process needs to be repeated). It's often so that the stage of anger is forfeited as a crowd redirects shame borne from their lack of courage onto one taking up what's worthy of emulation. There are many instances where the abrasive forces of rage are compelled to answer to pseudo-pacifistic majorities, but the reality of the human creature's inclination to shroud every modicum of pleasant life in unforgiving, hellish darkness — is that if it isn't put to deliberate use, it will leak out from whichever facet of oneself is least attended to.

Instead of being used to mow down the obstacles stalling progression — very often that energy is turned inward, and in an attempt to stifle discord, the world's inhabitants eviscerate themselves from the inside out. It's not optional to note that that anger is meant to serve as a *temporary* catalyst, as described earlier — then employed with precision thereafter only when one's garden is fatally threatened. The case for letting fear and anger go as one progresses is demonstrable in the product of a child, plant, or animal, raised with either as the principal sustenance to encourage growth.

3

A CURIOUS TRUST

There is one game for each person. So many permutations for proceeding exist that it isn't remotely feasible to expect even two to experientially integrate any set of principles in an identical fashion. Part of what makes a mob the powerful force it is, is the distance its members place between themselves, and the prospect of questioning any mutual participants; the amount of ignorance one is expected to tolerate to the end of acting in most groups is incalculable. Curiosity itself is an acknowledgment that the world can be split into many portions — which is why between foes questions are used as the stabbing instruments they essentially are, and why between friends it's such rare and precarious territory where direct, personal inquiry can happen.

The whole of science gets away with questioning things from every angle because the scientific method is more or less that approach's gamification. If one wonders whether, given its proneness to cause social abrasion, that act of looking deeper is not intrinsically valuable — see anything one holds dear which is simultaneously the product of technological innovation as proof. It's the incisive, questioning apparatus of mind which permits space for new growth to happen.

The precursor to development of any variety is always destructive, which is part of the reason those trusted as scholars, meant to regularly take up and make use of the scalpel of inquiry — are put through various culturally established vetting processes before their conclusions are permitted to be taken seriously. This is not to say the average person isn't capable of digging deeper or with more integrity than those intellectually pedestalized members of society — only that what they manage to unveil necessarily graces the front pages of mass perception following the lot who've sacrificed their share to the entities governing access to the figurative printing presses, traditionally. Since there are no moral imperatives inherently barring the exercise of explorative inquiry, those most liberally licensed to carry it out are obligated to express that their intentions are cohesive with group values — otherwise the risk is run they'll wield their scalpels downward on some proximal limb of consensus reality their peers use for support. No social organization is precluded from the tendency to preserve itself by imposing limits on what kinds of questions get to be asked, for the same reason no human will voluntarily place themselves on the lively end of a revolver save for in situations so grave as to necessitate the erasure of everything they've built to that point — though to assert the precursory circumstances of such a quandary as ever being voluntarily undergone is understandably controversial.

The question of whether it's safe to ask questions is the first essential step into darkness, whose answer sets the precedent for one's entire attitude as they proceed through the mysterious corridors of experience. Notice that the answer to that initial inquiry is fundamentally something a person gets to decide, just as the heading a captain sets upon their maiden voyage is both at their discretion, and the initial condition for what waters they'll face ahead. Once the act is reckoned safe enough to set sail, and one exposes themselves to a possibly volatile situation — every step taken thereafter is another voluntary decision to flip the coin. The fear of being wrong is basically what makes it fun to keep pushing into new territory, and why a lack of risk-aversion characterizes both the highly successful and the dismal failures — though failure's true claws only really get their grip once one quits flipping the coin. Someone in materially dire straits who unflinchingly pulls the trigger with a clear gaze as they gun for what they desire is a ground-shakingly inspiring thing to behold, because it reveals in the raw tenacity living creatures possess some irreducible ability to give no quarter in the rejection of submission, no matter the conditions. Such a being swallows their mortality with no chaser, refusing the pointlessness involved in cowering before it, and so too the delusion of fancying it's irrelevant.

Having such steady bearing within reach each time one gets to work — it's no wonder those who appear to willingly sacrifice the most fly the farthest. It has very little to do with the direct exchange of "x" in return for "y"; the clarity of perception possessed by one who follows through in arbitrarily releasing their limitations taps into a demeanor toward life which is both totally tranquil and wholly unrelenting. History's greatest figures don't come across as self-assured because they know something anyone else doesn't, they come across that way because the possibility of appearing wrong is a thing they take in stride the same way they might take a morning shit, and yet that ease isn't allowed to impede their rigor. There is no transcending the threat of risk, only the ever-present opportunity to embrace it.

To harbor complete focus, one must achieve access to immaculate internal lubrication — lest they undergo the unpleasant psyche-splicing that transpires, for example, in the midst of procrastination. Uncompromising fluidity must seamlessly intermingle with near frantic energy. The criticality of total absorption has to do with the absence of any separate mental tyrant, dictator from on high, foreman barking from the cognitive catwalk — present to gratingly espouse the necessity of doing whatever it is one is doing. The difference between the ambiance of dancing thoughtlessly, versus being told to do anything one would rather not — in the middle of doing it, is a heaven versus Earth level dichotomy playing out entirely within the subtle domain of passive consciousness. No peace exists in an environment wherein the task at hand is extraneous to all the fulfilling things which could otherwise be undertaken — though it's not totally clear why people so frequently discover themselves in such predicaments to begin with.

The intrusion of "that which is mandatory" is wholly illusory. One is more than free to engage with anything they like, which is plenty to facilitate a life worth carrying out — it isn't as though possessions are a reliable gateway to pleasure, it's in the act that the jeweled facets of existence reveal themselves. More than that, though, an act attended with total abandon for everything else has the potential to yield rewards not only for oneself, but for everyone in the vicinity, as well. Not that it matters to one who's truly lost themselves in some pursuit — but the fruits borne of their undertaking possess inspiration as their enticing flesh, and seeds bound to sprout in holes dug with the similar attentiveness of an entire being. The fruits aren't even the reason to undergo the journey — it's what's sacrificed for their sake that brings one into contact with the point; the potential for reward is the allure, firstly, but that anticipated reward becomes secondary to what's acquired as it's forgotten in the hypnotic overrule of the task. Once that's experienced, the world transforms from a thing sparsely populated with objects onto which one may latch and derive enjoyment, to an intrinsically fulfilling landscape, decorated with an abundance of color and sweetness. The transformation, counterintuitive as it may seem — arrives *after* the commitment to instill focus in oneself, which is why the lot who delay action until some point that isn't right now, struggle for years while seemingly remaining the same.

The plight of the chronically stuck is that of the hunter who's neglected to take their rifle from its rack until after they've spotted game. Just as what trainwreck will ensue when one refuses to abide by the order of operations in mathematics — nothing worth mentioning can occur until the foundations for execution have been properly laid. This is too clear an impasse, though — if sheer confusion is the factor preventing such from happening, a steady application of intent will inevitably straighten out the situation the same way one sat with a tangled mass of cords is unlikely to do anything other than make tangible progress if their desire is truly to get them organized. With that understanding, arguing to establish logistical clarity with someone failing to change is not only just as disingenuous as the blame they've placed on whatever hurdles lie before them — but insulting to their intelligence. What's necessary to prevent the situation from further devolving into an emotional clusterfuck from that juncture, is hidden in the simple acknowledgment that the friction is not on account of the details of the matter at hand — but by an incompatible or unclear alignment with what the other person wants to happen, and the apparent contents of the near future if they keep progressing in the direction the matter's resolution would roll them in. This happens less with individuals who have a clearly defined personal trajectory, but regardless of anyone else's expectations — it's in those moments an individual can learn to develop such a trajectory, or at the very least breach a ripe occasion for exposure to the deeper merits of what's thereto gone unappreciated.

The dumbest thing that can happen is a development wherein neither party knows what they want for themselves, but clings to the other as though having two people with machetes haphazardly chopping through a jungle any which way could be anything other than a high-risk low-reward activity; though if the combined stupidity of each is really so substantial as to generate such a situation, it's likely that the figurative equivalent of a machete wound would be about the only stimulus sufficient to force them to orient seriously. Fatalistic as it sounds, it's actually a fantastic reason to do whatever one does with some conviction that it'll turn out however it needs to. It's in the extrapolation of the observation that considering the relatively minuscule mental ability of the other predatory mammals, they seem to operate with altogether less anxiety than the average person — that one sees the most rational passage through being they can muster is to bow to whatever inarticulable limits shackle the human organism, and move forward despite them.

Part of the reason it can be so frustrating to watch a person pathologically impose limits on themselves is because the amount of struggle they manage to experience is so preposterously disproportionate relative to how much space is constantly available before the line past which things become truly impossible (it can extend past death if one wishes), that it can almost feel like it has to be a joke. Maybe it's done because there's some romance perceived in the act of perpetually fighting some battle — but the length of time one binds themselves to a single devil, is equal to that that they bind themselves to a single level.

Only a cockroach accepts the evolutionarily static position granted by their ability to survive virtually anything without protest — human beings shine under wholly different circumstances.

Failure is the basis, the ground, the prima materia of the human condition, infinitely more than it is a phenomenon. If one defines failure as the inverse of success, and the latter only occurs in the infinitesimal nexus joining the shift of one specific condition to another, failure *is* the condition on both sides of that nexus. Being afraid of failure is like being afraid to walk on the ground, and no one should be surprised if they're laughed at for tripping over themselves trying to "avoid" it. To assume failure's temporal characteristics match those of success, is akin to misunderstanding that a video game is a microcosm of life insofar as it's played — *not* insofar as it's paused. As the protagonist of a singular ongoing circumstance, no luxury to step outside of it exists — i.e., the schemes and calculations carried out to "avoid" failure, are done so from within it.

People silently degrade themselves when they slide into whatever aspect of their life they've conceptualized as failing, because it feels completely normal and comfortable.

That's like freaking out for accidentally walking into one's own kitchen instead of out the front door — but on sheer account of it being called "the kitchen." The inability to discern that one's position is of inexhaustible leverage, combining the visceral repulsion of the type who refuses to see they stand on the ground they condemn, with the awareness of their constant contact with it, thereby concocting and consuming, ceaselessly, the shittiest cocktail conceivable — for being near-indescribably absurd, is a freakishly common position to be in. In the event one experiences the ground of being as, indeed, quite different characteristically from the glimmering promise of attainment (a glimmering promise is mostly what it is, sort of how the dopamine purge of an orgasm compared to its build-up takes place in a precious fraction of the time), but isn't bent on conveying that dynamic as exclusively tragic — it becomes feasible to move through it skillfully, progressively facilitating higher degrees of attainment, and with greater frequency. Testing an infinitude of approaches up whatever mountain one aspires to ascend becomes a possibility, because no road forward is posted with signs debasing its validity. The more preferentially amorphous one can render the world to themselves outside the point they're presently aiming for, the less shackled they are on their journey. To shoot properly, it's necessary to ascertain one's target from a broad perspective firstly, then blot out the extraneous as one rests into the position of execution.

Miyamoto Musashi abided this rationale sincerely, detaching his preference even from the sword he depended on for his duels — an extreme demonstration that the entirety beyond the objective serves one most effectively as a boundless selection of tools. There is real overlap between the potential instant of floundering indecision he was avoiding by not assigning sentiments to his weapons, and the interpretation of whole decades of one's past as indispensable, or detrimental, or anything other than a deposit of information from which footholds could be established. Among the many fronts whereupon freedom of advancement manifests by regarding the world as such, one enjoys a deep and fruitful reprieve from the structurally tit-for-tat moral force-feeding carried out both publicly and privately. Instead of quivering at every step that some transgression may have taken place, the whole abstraction of morality can be erased in favor of simply observing the present state of the law, digesting the implications of any deviation from it following one's intended course, and adjusting accordingly.

Irretrievable time is wasted in the conjecture (it is always conjecture) of the morality endemic to specific ways of being, as though every conceivable infraction isn't merely an abstract expression of larceny. To murder is to steal life, to rape is to steal the body, to deceive is to steal under the guise of trust; yet is every animal a murderer? Every mine shaft an altar to rape? Every promise of Santa Claus' arrival the same betrayal of trust principal to adultery? Lay the inquiry at a thousand pairs of feet and receive a thousand nuanced answers. Humanity has learned to confound the emotional response to the potential of retaliatory thievery at the hands of authority with some invisible superstructure thought to influence equally. That system then appears twisted, corrupt, and broken, when it doesn't mirror one's preferred boundaries — as though it weren't in place to serve the preferences of those whose hands it's in.

The whole territory of morality is nothing more than what's stumbled upon when the resources individuals use for themselves bite into what other entities have identified as "theirs." Prior to that point — every act of taking is just casually referred to as within the domain of regular life. The only relevant question pertaining to this subject is whether what one wants to take will overstep any limit past which the risk of having things taken from oneself arises — and whether one deems any such risks worth shouldering. This line, for everyone, ultimately changes with context — ergo the enormity of law books. Right and wrong are concepts bestowed upon phenomena according to the retaliatory capacities possessed by presences in the environment likely to register them as some form of theft. They're heuristic pain-management methods evolved from instinctual responses.

Notice the clarity with which transgressions are experienced, and the lack, conversely, with which "good" is experienced. On the whole, no one cares what anyone does so long as whatever it is isn't sowing discord — thus the argument that the world is legitimately mostly good; which exists in greater quantity — stars, or space? Mathematically, space is the clear answer, but experientially, the quality of the stars is such that they hoard all the attention for themselves, rendering the *actual* infinitude of the space surrounding them inconspicuous. Despite the dismissive simplicity with which morality has been painted here, the following *is* of pretty extreme importance.

To do a thing well, the greater the vacuum created within oneself, the better, because it serves as room to cultivate considerable amounts of energy to directionally discharge in the execution of a task; as that energy is released, or when it's released, the vacuum organically fills once more. What it fills with comes from somewhere, and if the splash is big enough — it's far from unlikely others are going to feel stolen from in one way or another. It's not meant to be discouraging, such instances transpire on microscopic scales all the time — and since the only real way to combat it is to become an example of one who's identified with as little as possible outside the practices one attends with thorough attention in the service of their own fulfillment, the petty, despite what they may pose on the contrary, deserve only pity.

It's an interesting predicament, because for one who lusts after much in every corner of their experience, it quite makes sense for their senses to flood with envy in the event someone in their vicinity suddenly appears to receive some grand bounty, *"who didn't even want/need it"* — ignorant to how much concern needs to be relinquished to create space for its arrival. Consider the following depiction: Two pairs of neighbors exist. The first neighbor of the first pair owns an orchard, and is pleased; the second owns one apple tree, and is displeased. The first neighbor of the second pair owns an orchard, and is displeased; the second owns one apple tree, and is pleased.

In either scenario, the variable causing displeasure rests in the perception of the displeased individual — because the material circumstances are interchangeable. Any number of details could be woven into the example, but basically the hurdle is *what one thinks they deserve*. A bounty can only register as inadequate insofar as the cultivation is predicated on its arrival, which is why on a very basic level humility is necessary for success. The word success in this context is not being used to denote any physically measurable substance, but merely the joy one takes in existing — for what else is there? It's quite secondary that those capable of rendering themselves humble tend to receive more; it's just that the probability of reaping worldly benefits skyrockets when one can do something on its own merit, i.e., without feeling as though they're being stolen from, in lieu of interrupting their own flow by constantly checking the clock and the calendar and how many milliliters of soup someone else has, for fear they're wasting their time on an inferior enterprise.

Something quite unfortunate that tends to happen is illustrated in the example of someone who abides the heavy workload one at ease with their plight appears to prescribe themselves, but with the agenda of becoming disproportionately blessed in the same way. Like the sustenance of the spoon's contents is disguised as an airplane to entice a child to eat, are the riches promised on the far side of hard work; the pathology being described is equivalent to that of a child who never learns the intrinsic value of food, and instead, ages at constant odds with the fact that the spoon and its contents aren't *actually* an airplane. It's in this absurd circumstance that old, rich, miserable people come into existence — and perhaps why suicide almost appears to be an occupational hazard among the highly successful. If there's any measure of idiocy, it's to what degree the accumulation of material wealth is positively correlated with misery — and why many are inclined to regard the western world, despite its abundance of possessions, as fundamentally insane.

This dichotomy is beautifully and consistently illustrated in the art of hip hop. Even with an abundance of riches, more sexual partners than one could dream of managing, and admiration flooding in from every angle — melancholy, aggressive, slighted overtones permeate the notes its foremost artists generate. It's the pinnacle of alchemy — taking the most inane aspects of a society and transmuting them into dynamic energy instead of allowing them to rot the foundations. Such is the creative endeavor — breathing life into dead matter and its figurative equivalents. Everything worth looking at is buried beneath the unassuming, requiring some flavor of faith and an untiring pickax to unveil.

The reason so many leaps and twists and varying flavors of inculcations of faith and methods with which humans attempt to definitively imbibe the "rationale" for existing, exist, is because the simplicity of the matter is such that it lies *below* language. Language as a technology *is* a system of signs — *pointing* in the direction of things. Aiming it at itself (discussing the nature of a reality whose essence is incommunicable) in the effort to explicate anything, is like executing a function in a programming language which executes itself, i.e., like setting off an infinite loop, and is why philosophers will never be out of work.

Some take the tack that if that's the case, there's either no value in analyzing the world's contents at all, or at least an absolute need to bind the practice to some secondary motivation. This, however, is like disparaging the value of music because despite everything the sounds *do*, they never, per se, *get* anywhere. Anyone who enjoys music understands how laughably indefensible such a take is, and extrapolated to the greater reality that the sun is likely to consume the Earth before anyone gets off it — anyone who enjoys *anything* understands how laughably indefensible such a take is.

4

A PRISTINE SENSE OF BALANCE

O ne enormous point of leverage that goes over people's heads are the implications proceeding from the fact that every modicum of reality bleeds into every other. Typically this presents itself with clarity in whatever domain one possesses expertise in; a politically minded individual is likely to discern the politics in things the opposite type of person would never dream of, just as a mechanic may be prone to seeing social dynamics generally perceived as fluid and organic through a lens revealing them as a quite measured, systematized set of phenomena. Firstly, the insight that everyone can only reason from within their personal territory, and is therefore predictable in their analyses, augments the net usefulness of one's perceptual inventory by no small extent.

To unlock it, though, one must relinquish the conception that the world is a thing only sufficiently describable in the terms one is personally familiar with. The most basic means to smash that vase is to observe the fact that over seven thousand spoken languages exist, yet everyone speaks of the same world. Practice in meditating on the *lack* of differentiation implied by the statement

"all things are unique," facilitates the development of eyes fit to see the world as a game of snakes and ladders, with an ever-increasing density of ladders. It becomes possible to shatter dogma in one's stride as a matter of course, without causing offense. It's a skill like any other, and understandably developed in service to whatever one is personally keen on achieving, but it truly does a lot to curb the landmines of strife and misunderstanding littering the space both inside and outside one's head, given they reflect one another. The playwright Terence's proclamation paints the attitude of the proficient in this vein succinctly:

"I am a human being; nothing human can be alien to me."

If observation alone isn't sufficient to clarify the inherently shifting nature of established boundaries as a quite traversable inter-tidal zone of sorts, one can exercise themselves in the following manner: Consider that upon entering dreamless sleep, during the period one's consciousness is deleted as thoroughly as it might be in death — the whole world is deleted by extension, then conjured again upon waking. If it's too far a stretch, consider that one's unique experience of perception is fundamentally irreplicable, then follow that implication to the domain wherein the whole phenomenon of deriving information on a scientific basis, or on *any* basis, is a thing that occurs *inside* oneself. I.e. — follow it into a place where the outer limit of the universe and the outer limit of oneself, *are literally one and the same limit.*

From that point — shift attention to the incalculable enormity of the situation one presently finds themselves in, until that self feels as a laughable mote of nothingness in the ineffably vast sea of happening. See that at every scale, from the minutiae of one's hand to the outer reaches of the sky, the horizon recedes so infinitely far that the relative presence of oneself ceases to be so much as remotely coherent. Rock back and forth between these perspectives frequently enough, and it becomes a cakewalk to conceptually place oneself in any pair of shoes without so much as a hair of disingenuity.

To say each facet of experience bleeds into every other isn't quite up to par with actuality; it's that from every point, every other point is potentially accessible based on the agility with which one can swap perceptual lenses, and also that the perspectives adjacent to whichever new angles are taken become increasingly available in the same way a sunrise would if one decided to sleep outside. Discomfort is so inevitable in the initial attempts that it's actually safe to aim one's crosshairs at discomfort itself if no insight to this point has been imparted. The reason that's the case is because to shift the context wherein the world as presently understood is defined, is to uproot oneself from whatever facts affirm one's place in it.

Intrinsic to each are varying levels of tolerance for this particular kind of nomadism, and it's true a balance exists between that practice, and the planted assurance afforded by any given perceptual home, so to speak. In all cases, whether the circumstances are static or dynamic, those composing the present foundation from which some undertaking is initiated ought eventually be sacrificed in service to it; onto one who commits themselves intently to anything, the obligation to fulfill that rite of passage is inevitably thrust. The reason is because for any system to be maximally exalted, opposing conditions are necessary in its refinement — as in honing a sword, the opposing sides of the blade demand a balance of attention, else it will cut inconsistently; or in exercise, that gains require a finely attended ratio of work to rest. The resistance, typically, in exposing oneself to their inverse tendencies, is in two illusions.

The first is a distortion of the fact that where one walks is fundamentally lacking in some way. That isn't to say establishing a *negative* relationship with one's present condition is necessary — only an appreciation of its transience, and subsequently an orientation at some other point in the distance. The second is in doubting the efficacy with which change will facilitate growth, generally manifesting as some application of the logic that since any new conditions couldn't be nailed down definitely, i.e., are antithetical to security — they can have no value. Presented as such, or in any other way, the human brain has, for all intents and purposes, a boundless repository of ammunition wherefrom rebuttals to either accusation can be made to reinforce the sanctity of whatever position one presently occupies, constructed on the basis of sheer instinct.

Consider the following: The rational instruments of mind are not prerequisite for self-preservation — but extensions of processes functioning to that end. Since the human creature is capable of extending its identity into any domain language can be wrapped around — the same knee-jerk, fight or flight responses carried out by the lower brain can be and are regularly executed under the guise of rational discernment. The most imposing edifice of this phenomenon is legalese, which serves no purpose other than to obfuscate its own vulnerabilities and exploit those laid bare in the chinks of other, lesser legalese, to the end of establishing and maintaining security.

In other words, a person's intelligence as it's traditionally understood has nothing to do with their capacity to level up, which is a pain in the ass for everyone who's spent their days accumulating information to the end of self-defense — because they curse themselves with the gift of being able to cogently repudiate every justification for undergoing transformative change. Such is the plight of miserable intellectuals who mistake the walls of their prospective sepulcher as useful while they still walk the Earth. Conversely, and perhaps most tragically, they contain within themselves the potential to expertly navigate what new territories they refuse to enter. It requires some seriously high-octane mental agility to precisely ascertain the basis upon which a given argument for change rests, deduce the weak points of the emotional beams supporting it, then employ the exact means of demolition necessary to implode the whole thing while maintaining a front of indifference. It's like watching someone use an F1 race car to hit twenty thousand revolutions per minute at a standstill for the sake of scaring squirrels out of their yard.

In a sense it's difficult to imagine where the hangup often is with those possessed of such apparently high tier capacities — but the greater reality is that they've likely placed so much energy into the job of developing the electronics and farkles of the ship they're governing, that they've bled themselves of any concern with respect to navigation. It's understandable — the bigger and more complex the ship, and the longer one has been traveling along a singular course, the higher the perceived risk involved in steering it in all its mass and glory toward some new, potentially dangerous frontier. That, and any reputation for competence one has developed in the use of their familiar methods, voluntarily oriented in a direction other than where there definitely aren't maelstroms waiting to swallow it in its entirety, is a special kind of Russian roulette only played by those with nothing to lose.

It's true, the specific pathology being discussed will most readily call to mind images of the ancient and cognitively crystallized — as it goes, there are the old and the bold, but none both old and bold. It would be irresponsible to incite upheaval in an individual whose path serves them perfectly well, though it's arguable nothing would be incited in spite of anyone's best efforts in one for whom that's actually the case. In refuting the argument this way, however, it's demonstrated in no trivial manner that whatever directives hold the most potential for catalyzing growth, are only ultimately revealed as such to each individual with respect to themselves, hence the obliteration of the excuse that there's no way to tell where to go or what to do.

Just because another cannot reveal one's own path directly does not indicate its absence (otherwise where from has one come?) — only that its details, available to oneself, may be concealed from the outside by whatever foliage defines its edges. It's a matter of individual responsibility to ascertain the optimal means of proceeding, not on any moral basis, but simply because no one else possesses the faculties to do so. The best one can hope for in the way of deriving clarity at the hands of another is only to the extent actions taken in cooperating with them align with one's own trajectory. Deliberately acting beyond what overlap lies there effaces precious time — though there are instances where one may uncover an objective worth pursuing to the point of death, which happens to be in direct service to another.

No merit lies in projecting blame in the event of a perceived obstruction; all external factors merely exist as inert geographical features as far as is useful in the context of one's journey — if they're to be regarded with anything aside from passive appreciation. Somewhat paradoxically, this also includes one's own thoughts and emotions. As the compass with which each next step is ascertained, no instance of either can conscionably be placed out of favor without detracting from the intelligibility of their indications. That is to say, *aiming away* from any particular thought or emotion will gradually lock one into a vicious cycle, because as the context they're called forth in changes, varying responses in relation to them become appropriate.

Imagine that one heads east toward an intended location, simultaneously holding onto a distaste for the cardinal direction west — then establishes a second destination based on what information they've gathered from their voyage and arrival to their new current position. As they start off, they'll find that the thoughts and emotions (west) they ran from to reach the point they're *now* heading from, are at a new angle. This is totally normal — the problem arises when instead of staying the course, some amount of influence from their initial labeling as "inherently to be avoided" displaces one's point of aim. In the initial stages of the habit, one will shoot slightly wide of their intended destination, then, finding themselves circumventing their intent by progressively greater margins as they increasingly associate "west" with the developing problem — one may eventually discover themselves in a position where what they truly desire appears to be completely and utterly at odds with what they believe they "should" desire. This is how a personality splits in half, or manifests at intervals extreme expressions of what might be considered mutually exclusive worldviews.

This can start right off the bat if one is punished as a child for emoting, or communicating certain thoughts, instead of for carrying out certain actions. The more one struggles to abandon their feelings in the passage of time, the more critical it becomes to forthrightly embrace them.

Love is a thing inextricably linked to the propagation of life. From an evolutionary perspective — the assertion of which dictates which proceeds in the order of the latter, and then the former. Experientially, though, it's more honest to assert that the end in propagating life is to engender love, given the immense pain of childbirth, and freakishly confounding challenge of child-rearing — to say nothing of what's sacrificed in reaching a point where those pills begin to appear feasibly swallowed. Perhaps no greater sympathy is mustered in the human organism than in the event of a fellow person's flirtation with obliteration as part of the collateral collected in some unwitting withdrawal of love.

As the baseline example for illustrating love's dynamics, it's a wonder why where it's sought outside the domain of interpersonal relationships, the extrication of pain from the process of getting one's hands on it would be expected to any degree. In the analysis of human accomplishment on the whole, it's perfectly reasonable to draw the conclusion that every institution ever created has been established to the end of facilitating situations which forcibly squeeze select chemicals from the brain; why, when their densest organic synthesis only occurs in tandem with overwhelming agony, wouldn't every other thing involving them imply some correlating instance of pain?

Every undertaking is either carried out for the sake of something that'll make it worth it, or enjoyed at some expense; they're essentially the same statement. The space where the most time is spent, where there is an apparent qualitative equilibrium, is the place from which the decision of what game to play next, should be made. Early in life it's normal to place oneself in pleasant situations at unknown cost — then gradually try one's hand at preemptively calculating the risk to reward ratio involved with what gratification one casts themselves upon. The issue over time is actually the same feeling that one's been blindsided; it's likely the anticipated harvest won't be reflected in actuality.

The majority of individuals repeatedly manage this destruction of expectation, shifting between it and the intermittent indulgence in a guaranteed short-term dose of goods — whose effects the body is primed to interpret as justification for tackling some ensuing trauma. The wisest approach requires a certain amount of faith that the structure of enjoyment is as such. Notice that in the first type, one selects their cake at a random price (any combination of cake and poison, chosen frequently enough, assimilate themselves into one's equilibratory state), and in the second instance, one falls for the illusion that they choose their particular cake in exchange for whatever path promises its redemption.

If one is willing to simply accept whatever cake awaits, placing expectations to the side, they unlock the option of being able to select, and subsequently master the consumption of, their own poison. At hand with this option is a certain aspect of clarity — inaccessible with the intimation of pain on the horizon, or with expectations strangling one's spirit as they move in what they hope to be the direction they'd like to go. Developing in the course of time, should one opt to swing hard either way, is a progressive blunting of one's sensitivities in relation to it — i.e., one who attempts to use each moment as a means of directly ingesting pleasure, makes themselves increasingly sensitive to the experience of displeasure, and vice versa.

The pleasure principle — that all creatures do the things they do in an effort to experience pleasure and avoid pain, rings true with humans no less than it does with the simplest organisms. Its contrary aspect, "the reality principle," exists to account for the uniquely human ability to assess, and act accordingly with respect to, the future. Nothing about the reality principle contradicts the pleasure principle in humans, however — it's only that the means of acquiring pleasure people use vary depending on how they cognize time. When speaking to someone about the future who's locked into a cycle of cashing-in on instant gratification, the habituated process they've adopted as the means to make themselves feel okay, will, in their conception, render what's beyond their next fix as approaching mythological. To acknowledge the possibility of moving in an innately beneficial direction, is to insert oneself into boiling water as far as someone incapable of projecting the image of themselves beyond the present moment is concerned, because the only tangible implication is the masochism they'd need to embody to initiate such a pattern of being.

It is arguably a human's highest pinnacle to live in a rhythm of continuous effort while consciously postponing the reception of pleasure to a point beyond the finality of their own existence. The idea of this type of person is so absurdly homogeneous as a culturally encouraged figure to replicate that it requires a deliberate foray into the thralls of hedonism to even begin assimilation into the sector of phenomena one is ignorant to, and the sacrifice involved in such a foray, undergone on a consistent enough basis — humanity itself. From this angle, the human creature is a thing designed to traverse the boundary of instinct — the unspeakably contrasting emergence of incalculable evolutionary developments, all apparently pursuing downright petty quantities of pleasure in comparison, given its willingness to throw itself into abhorrent disharmony for the sake of its ends.

Earth's crown problem child; the only entity so inconsolably at odds with its existence that the prospective feat of productively replicating the nuclear fusion reaction normally only feasible in the conditions native to stars — the closest example being one million times larger and somewhere in the neighborhood of one-hundred-seventy-five times hotter on average than their home planet, not to mention ninety-four million miles away (information unto itself inconceivably far past the perceptual grasp of a single other organism present on it, despite its trivial accessibility to humans), was made a thing of the past as of Monday, December 5, 2022, thirteen days prior to the date of this transcription. The concept that the territory every living thing instinctually seeks to avoid is probably within the range of unimpressive conscious accessibility to an intent enough human should not be even remotely questionable in light of that.

Neither, then, is the ability to deliberately edit one's internal state in the calibration of one's faculties en route to some specific end. It's uninteresting enough to propose that one's internal state is reflective of their external circumstances — but in that statement's reversal, and subsequently the inversion of which half possesses the qualitatively subjective aspect, one gains direct access to dangerous amounts of their potential. In its regular form, there's the assumption that the internal state *depends* on external circumstances, the same way the image on a body of water's surface could be said to depend on the sky for its contents. Notice, however, in that observation, it's merely that the water possesses no means to position itself of its own accord, and so reflects at the mercy of the sky's shifting picture. The internal human state need not necessarily be imprisoned that same way.

Consider the following: One's external circumstances are reflective of their internal state. Is it not so that the mind contains therein such substantial dynamism that the matter of whether it itself, or what it observes, holds the throne regarding which reflects at the mercy of which, is at the very least indeterminate? Firstly, consider that at the baseline of experience there exists the Hard Problem of Consciousness — making it impossible to directly refute in any way the proposition of epistemological solipsism. From there, experiment with shifting one's concept of what the world fundamentally is, in various ways. Consider that it is the internal organ of some enormous celestial being, or a dream, or a dance, or the projection of some observable entity within it. It becomes feasible, with thorough attention, to *experience* the world as factually being a thing predicated on the principles characterizing any arbitrary adjustment of one's own mind.

The inability to willfully influence the contents of the physical world with ease, as one might their own limbs, is merely the equal opposite restriction to the world's inability to bend the human spirit any particular way — just as neither a cat nor its reflection in the mirror have the upper hand over the other. Extreme examples of each cap ranges from the strongmen and the paralyzed, and also from the agoraphobic to those capable of unflinchingly immolating themselves in public. The upper limits of worldly restriction, oddly, overlap with the upper limits of its perceptual malleability, i.e., the end result of the heaviest restrictive measure carried out by a government in the binding of one to solitary confinement, is the same as that of one who's taken their course of spiritual attainment into its final stages — complete societal isolation and a position of stillness assumed; the conditions enveloping one who's made themselves into a thing requiring maximal worldly intervention, are the same as those enveloping one who's made the world into a thing requiring minimal personal intervention. The stark dichotomy between the internal states of these two individuals clarifies that the apex of human inertia which they both approach the physical embodiment of — i.e., death, characteristically brings the lot of phenomena into union, and perhaps conversely that life as a force is insatiably divisive and complexifying. A fascinating insinuation of these apparently conflicting properties is that each may in fact be striving to replicate the qualities of the other. Life, an irreparably incompressible explosion of sorts — breeds what it does in patterns, as a rule. Assuming it could develop in some singular, unvarying manner — it would be in its propagation indistinguishable from the void of space, the emptiness of unconsciousness, and the bleak nothing of death. It may be unwittingly struggling in spite of some fundamental inability to help itself out of contrast, to manifest in the unlimited fashion of its truly boundless opposite. On that opposite hand, it's those mutually indistinguishable expressions of yin wherefrom the enormous, irreplicable pulsations of the discernible, spring. Each human wakes for the first time following what's only describable as a sleep they never recollect having entered into. The womb of phenomena as such is formless, yet spews from itself, nature.

To elaborate on the specific mechanism by which things emerge is merely to carry the dissecting operation out upon the walls wherein their emergence occurs — i.e., to dice fruitlessly at the edges in an attempt to see *where* it's all coming from. Funnily enough, the empty space presented when a thing is severed, *is* the answer. This is evident even as the basis of one's wildest imaginative exploits in the effort to extricate matter from the void — "some" can only exist in the presence of none, otherwise the lack of contrast forces whatever's there to recede into the ever-present nil wrapped around everything. Notice how the excessive density of various metropolitan areas tends to assume a certain quality of emptiness; chocked so full with sensory stimuli, their perceptible impact fades into an incoherent amalgam like so many colors blended on canvas with too heavy a hand, upon which only the loudest and most extreme make any mark.

What's most fascinating about this is that in such an environment — the yin and the yang switch polarities, because everyone's attention gravitates to the quaint, hidden away spaces wherefrom the crowd can be escaped. In other words, silence becomes immensely impactful when there's an over-saturation of noise, and so the passive aspect of existence can really be described, at the highest level, as that which there is the most of locally.

As the observer zooms-out, the pinpoint whereto attention is called disappears, and its substrate becomes the medium of some new contextual frame — the inverse proceeding in the event of the observer zooming-in. That is to say, anything outstanding can be deleted in one of two ways; one can subject themselves to it until it becomes boring, or divorce themselves from it to such a degree that it ceases to be relevant. In light of this — it's the case that the most persistently affective things to one are those with which they're neither overly concerned with, or extraordinarily distanced from. It's with this information that one develops the capacity to deliberately determine the background, foreground, and focal point(s) of their life, because the frequent misinterpretation is that the focal point is synonymous with the foreground, which renders one prone to encountering an impasse, for example, in eliminating their lover from the legitimate realm of personal importance just as much as they might if they were to outright abandon them — by unabashedly showering them with all their time and attention. A pristine sense of balance is needed to make anything wondrous.

5

A Helical Phenomenon

The reason it's so tricky to verbally entrap the optimal approach in anything is because the terms at hand can only indicate the polarities, and thus are regularly in a state of division from the event of fluid dynamism before the point past which they themselves evolve into an irreplicable art form of a sort. The most coherent, captivating speeches, though attended with nodding and encouragement as though the words being spoken are stolen directly from the innards of each audience member — are sensational precisely because to execute an impactful speech is an uncommon feat. The nectar is traceable in its emergence to the rate at which an erratic, shifting system, possessed of uncomplimentary aspects, vibrates

— transforming via those constituent relationships into something generally recognizable for its beauty, in lieu of its repulsiveness.

The most perfect example of this is sex. For starters, it can only be intently spoken of for so long in awkward, lopsided declarations see-sawing from the scientific to the emotionally poetic before the situation at hand evolves into the act itself — and then there's the point that its individual aspects isolated out of context are quite distinctly odd and somewhat unsavory. Not only does everything worth giving one's attention operate like this, but there's the unique attunement each has in respect to the systems they're most familiar with which breeds varying dimensions of appreciation within them. Some are attuned to sex to such a degree that they more or less smell it approaching on the horizon like a motorcyclist will perceive the distinct "po-ta-to" cadence of a cold started Harley as unmistakably that, where a stranger to the nuances of those particular realms will merely sense their subtleties as indistinct features of the environment — until the one is nearly to home base, or the other is at least within eyeshot.

It's a mechanic which should incite optimism, because it means boredom is effectively remedied through thorough attention. There's not necessarily a need to remove oneself from one's endeavor for a breather when there's an unending descent into the details of every piece of reality lying in wait to be appreciated. The risk run is merely that one places themselves in rarefied solitude when they delve incessantly enough into anything.

People often become discouraged because they're convinced everything's been done, but the reality is merely that the mine shaft of human accomplishment is substantially more cavernous than it once was as a byproduct of this type of delving. It isn't as though shortcuts to the current frontiers don't exist, and it isn't necessary to personally do the work of one's predecessors — merely to appreciate what's been developed and carry forth the torch from the supports of the most recently blown-out threshold leading into whichever domain excites one most fervently. After chasing a thing so far in a given direction, describing it as work almost becomes disingenuous, as it undergoes the shift from a thing carried out in conflict with habit, knowledge, and instinct, to a largely unobtrusive feature of one's reality which can be effortlessly attended the same way as personal hygiene.

That isn't to say the meat of one's vocation won't present itself with challenges scaling relative to one's abilities, but that the capacity to initiate the interaction with it will cease to be obstructed by hesitation — initiation being, in anything, the most elusive point of engagement. That's so, because until one develops the prowess necessary to kick up a worthy pattern in any particular domain, one's involvement with it must begin on either of the aforementioned ends of a gracelessly balanced undertaking. It's a life of ceaseless toil to possesses the habit of starting up progress in some direction, then scrapping it in favor of something new. Whether or not the thing is socially conducive, financially rewarding, or what one's parents desire for them — progressing only to the point of minimal proficiency before taking on some new endeavor renders it remarkably difficult across time to see *anything* through to its end, though maybe the recalcitrance involved in forfeiting mastery is to avoid becoming dependent on it — favoring instead the skill of picking up and using any tool with the briefest possible learning curve.

It's also reasonable to assert that it's a misuse of terms to say anything *could* be carried out to its end, because the conditions any end is defined in relation to are more or less arbitrarily imposed. One could say the best line to draw to indicate the end of a thing is one past which entirely new phenomena emerge — but upon careful inspection it's revealed a fissure located anywhere in a given pattern will unfailingly be interpretable as such a place. It's the case that there are many ends which hide in plain sight within seamlessly spliced stretches of inactivity. For example, the halfway point traversed in a journey across the ocean, though sensorily imperceptible without the aid of navigatory instruments, spells the end of the stretch where it would be more resource-efficient to turn back home, and the beginning of that in which a strong follow-through takes precedence as the economically superior course of action.

Though physical occurrences often transpire in a cyclical fashion — no two cycles are identical, and so a more accurate statement would be that they transpire in something resembling a helix. It's useful to regard any chapter of experience through this particular lens of progression, because it highlights the opportunity to use the past as an orienting marker, while simultaneously buffering one against the trap of becoming identified as intractably stuck inside some insidious repetition of events. It's possible that nature happens on the basis of wholly predetermined cycles, novelty being the illusion produced as the ones which close over the course of imperceptibly enormous lengths of space-time disturb the order of the smaller, more tangible ones — but ultimately, to concern oneself beyond the point of amusement with such possibilities is a waste of energy.

The potential coordinates of the dichotomy between fate and free will, should, no matter what insinuations one may manage to make themselves privy to regarding their balance, be honored as just that — a potential dichotomy. Going out of one's way to inquire which is dominant is already demonstrative of a fatal misunderstanding — because either the question is posited with the use of one's personal volition, which negates determinism, or it's posited as an expression of an inscrutable, universal predetermination; asking the question, in other words, simply provides insufficient purchase to pry behind the problem. For such matters whose details would, if digested, place the knowledge of the entire mechanism of existence within one's grasp in a way that would eliminate the necessity for wonder, one should simply observe the potentials as an exercise, as opposed to becoming identified with their pursuit, or worse yet, with any conclusions regarding them. It's crucial in the maintenance of sanity that one only attempts to apprehend the limits of the universe to a degree in proportion with their personal limits — otherwise they subject themselves to psychological and existential fires they may not be remotely proofed for. Perhaps there's no need to append the disclosure that the risk associated with any given line of inquiry is the complete responsibility of the individual carrying it out — however, not only do the full extent of those risks vary drastically from person to person, but so too the appreciation that there are any risks at all.

The disconnects, actually, are so massive in this respect that if one finds others reacting to their native interests or predilections with abject terror, or any indication that they belong on the other side of the fence excluding that which isn't realistically manageable, even and especially to the point of treating one as pathological — the only credence displayed in the service of their amelioration should merely be to the end of getting them off one's back. To have anything express itself in one to such a degree that it seems alien is not only an indication that there's oil lying under the surface in its vicinity waiting to be struck, but that there's a vacuum of oil for a radius of miles. There's no more efficient way to intercept the ceiling of one's potential than with one's skull, sat atop some irrepressible geyser of a tendency — nor is there a more reliable way to gauge the potential pressure therein, than in assessing the dearth of such geysers in one's locality.

Opportunities nested in the unscratchable itches of one's personality are bastards to pinpoint as such when there's shame associated with them on account of one's peers' insistence they're contraindicative to the acceptably prescribed course of existence. Self-acceptance isn't a prerequisite for progress because it should be used to try skipping the line of attainment and pedestalize oneself, it's a prerequisite because it's the only means of getting a full grip of where one's standing — and it would be a travesty to develop into a reasonably adept something or other while walking to and from work upon veins of gold. Accessible to each are deposits of information completely fenced off from outside perception on the sole basis that people inhabit separate bodies, and thus proceed through separate territories — there's so much sensitivity in a single human being that even the difference in experience between two identical twins raised "the same" could hardly be overstated.

It is always a mistake to assume others understand where one is coming from. To become totally offended or enthralled in response to anyone's criticism or praise, is to wholly confound their experience with one's own, despite the fact that those two things are imperfectly overlaid. It's critical to clarify for oneself why one seeks the opinions of others, because without that anchor, the influence taken on loses its potential to reveal any superior courses of action — bombarding, instead, everything resting upon whatever incomparable foundations their perspective necessarily annihilates in the assumption that it's personally applicable. There's no need to polemically retaliate against every other perspective as it's regarded — just to appreciate its arrival while attempting to discover what wisdom it may possess relative to that which one presently undergoes.

Since everyone derives their conclusions from irreplicable bases — it's valuable to note that to all of them, another's inability to proceed without permission or encouragement is indicative of a fatal flaw. There is no more discouraging a trait in one with whom another expects to be cooperating, than to find any deposit of superficially copied external opinions, including one's own, dictating the moves they make before some tangible amount of low level reasoning and subsequent action has taken place. For one to be so avoidant of making mistakes that they stall the undertaking of any action whatsoever in favor of rumination pending an apprehendable green light, is to confound the principal usefulness in possessing a machine as complex as the human brain with that of a paperclip. On the contrary — it can be a source of immense frustration to deal with an individual hell-bent on implementing some basically inadequate solution in the execution of a task, not because they're actually necessarily incompetent, but because they rabidly defend the pretense that they've precisely gauged the parameters of the problem at hand.

In either scenario, notice that the deciding factor in overcoming the given barrier has nothing to do with the impartment of any specific information — but merely that one divorces themselves from the conception that a solution is ever something trapped inside a person, whether in someone else, or oneself. One will attend, as close to the root as possible, the problems they're concerned with solving; to assume someone's attitude is a problem is not only to completely neglect that fact, but disrespect, and subsequently layer more problems on top of, an individual who's expressing whatever they are in response to the stimuli they're maximally capable of concerning themselves with in a given instance.

The matter of honesty is immensely confusing, not only because it's defined in accordance with eight-billion separate perspectives, but perspectives on a world that's constantly undergoing various types of change. There's also the matter that since the means of communicating reality at the most basic levels imaginable, whether to oneself or to others, are acts of unavoidably imperfect translation — it's not clear to what extent anyone is capable of being honest. By definition, honesty is synonymous with sincerity, and denotes an absence of deceit.

It does not, however, take very much investigation to discover that the many terms used to delineate what's real from what isn't, circle themselves in a wide ouroboros; to deceive is to misrepresent the truth, the quality or state of being true means to be in accordance with reality, reality is defined as the world or the state of things as they actually exist, and "actually," finally, is defined as the truth of a situation. All assessments of the world, then, as it honestly truly really actually is — are based on tautology, i.e., on data obtained from an inescapable net of kind people who all give coordinates to one of their own in response to a request for directions. Facetious as it sounds, there's no way to conclusively *say* anything about what's going on when one screams bloody murder to

"PEPPER SPRAY THE FUCKING MOUNTAIN LION PLEASE FOR THE LOVE OF GOD —" so why does that exclamation confer what needs to happen in order to instigate the situation's return to equilibrium, or even paint a cohesive picture at all? Inductively reliable sensory input associated with each part of the phrase. That, however, is not a luxury at hand in the analysis of any statement which does not assume one's familiarity with the stimuli in question.

Deception, then, is the deliberate misrepresentation of a rift in the cohesive understanding of stimuli. This established, is it not so that there's a primary act of deceit in every initial transference of information? If truth, as gathered to this point, is only constructed insofar as there's mutual appreciation for a thing in and of itself — does not any expectation that another ought to take on one's perspective erroneously prime that other to perceive their own as characteristically inadequate? Not to suggest that's inherently transgressive, but if it's the case, at the very least it's fair to observe there's an ongoing dance of sorts between each shifting clump of verbiage, whereupon people place chips touting their representative clump as most eminently descriptive of bedrock reality — just as soon as they move to speak. It would place into perspective as well the woe surrounding a child's "programming" as they rise through the various tiers of social assimilation — it's not as though their uncultured perceptions would be any less accurate than those of an adult, merely that their corresponding attitudes toward things are as-of-yet etched.

The enterprise of human communication is hilarious because there's a positive correlation between the digestible mass of information, and the fragmentation in the collective grasp of what's going on. Shifting attention into the social sphere, largely what breeds success is the ability to absorb the world as communicated through various perspectives without abrasively grating them against the finer details of one's own — one's prowess in managing this externally, growing in relation to the capacity to peaceably regard their own internal paradoxes.

In consideration of haywire family gatherings wherein incendiary political or religious discourse takes place, note the divisions are often so deeply entrenched that the only rational assessments at hand to make sense of them involve disparaging the fundamental character of one's own kin. This is exceedingly unfortunate; whatever standpoint one's opposition across the ambrosia salad is taking, is *just wrong* — it's in direct contravention to the honest, true, real, actual situation. This approach does nothing but perpetuate alienated feelings and accelerate the festering of whatever wounds have been spitefully inflicted upon one another, unless it's done in good spirits as a sort of intellectual sparring, or minimally with the active intent of meeting at an unseen junction someplace in the distance. (Keyword "unseen" — not attempting to lure someone into a premeditated conclusion with a front of innocence.) To one involved in such fuckery, the suggestion is not to shut up, smile, and nod — it's to take the time on one's own to bathe, fully, in contemplation of why to that other person the information ("misinformation," if that's as much as can be swallowed) they're holding onto is such an investment for them, without jumping to conclusions. Since the world necessarily reveals itself as paradoxical when observed from multiple angles, hard-gazing at it from one is not sufficient to any end save exacerbating the frustration in trying to pin it in place as a wholly digestible entity come the mildest intimation of its variance. Spinning it as something conceivable in a dangerously foreign light will enormously reduce the degree to which its presentation as such comes as a threat, and render it feasible to open lines of communication with those previously painted as inaccessible on account of their outlook.

The notion that on account of one's own experiences, another's ignorance precludes any mutual ground from being established — is as absurd as becoming personally frustrated with a child for being at odds with some matured perspective, only with the added insult that the subject is likely grown. The facade that personal affliction or experience is justification for invalidating another is a horrific misuse of pride — one becomes like a "teacher" who teaches nothing, but instead parades about, droning on of what enlightened knowledge they would bequeath if only their peers were wise enough to handle it. In any case, the act of deliberately offsetting oneself from the direct path of another's comprehension is always a matter of insecurity, because the only reason to sincerely engage in subterfuge is in self-defense. It's not an act of submission to be above returning the favor in the event of an encounter with one who operates as such — but a refusal to disrespect oneself, or the wounded bird, in mimicking its shuffling display.

The best way to approach one like this is to suspend the disbelief that they're speaking out of their ass, listen attentively, and resist the urge to mockingly patronize their persona. It's the avoidance of this latter type of criticism which sparks the pattern of behavior causing the individual's repeated encounter with it in the first place, like habitually speeding past the cops in an underwhelmingly fast car so as to duck them after having been needlessly hemmed up one too many times; a few pleasantly tame encounters are required to draw any confounding hackles back down and into proportion with the situation. This could be imagined an inefficient way to cope, with one's inward focus appearing as that which would rationally take precedence — but in any case there's that requirement. Despite what's been conveyed, no degree of situational rectification can come to pass unless one personally explores which avenues relative to the issue presenting itself would make possible the alleviation of experienced congestion — and that exploration is basically a thing undergone from wherever one personally stands. The presentation of the aforementioned considerations is merely to exemplify what interpretive frames can be made available so as to create space to proceed gracefully and with minimal discord, which require nothing to access save some appreciation of validity across the spectrum of human experience.

To clarify what's been established for the sake of the following point: any assertion of "new" information with the aim of eradicating whatever occupies the relevant perceptual inventory space of those it's presented to, is deceptive in that it preemptively ousts a latent concept in favor of an entirely different one — rather than earnestly attending to the discovery of some linguistic middle ground. The types who carry this out most rampantly and insensitively are those who believe themselves above duplicitousness, because they've honed their speech and manner such that the thought of acting deceptively comes across quite potently as beyond their conception. It takes no rocket scientist to see why such a personality serves as a breeding ground for the tendency toward misrepresentation to prosper unchecked.

Comparatively, it's substantially more reasonable to interface with one who's forthright about the paint they use to favorably influence others' perspectives — because they lay the possibility forth plain as day, eliminating the expectation of adherence to some unspoken code of truthfulness in favor of intelligible boundaries past which it's freely disclosed no cooperation should be expected. Respecting one to whom the idea that their own behavior is structurally such that it moves to obfuscate the validity of others', appears outrageous — to understate their proneness to doing exactly that, is usually alarmingly easy. It's so that the only means they make available to themselves to the end of cooperation, are coercive; in their efforts to engage interpersonally without consciously herding people in line with their expectations, it becomes their unconscious baseline of conduct — they eliminate the potential space prior to the deliberate deployment of manipulation by forcing themselves to use it as a starting point, just as the only color anything happens to reflect corresponds with that singular wavelength it refuses to absorb.

In consideration that the reality of deceit is untraceable, it's possible such individuals are fully conscious of their effect, and embody it deliberately. The suspicion of it being mostly accidental comes from a parallel drawn with the tendency to embarrassingly enact some loathsome behavior in subconscious self-flagellation as a response to failed attempts at stifling desire. For example, coming across as demanding with the seller of something one "caved" to purchasing. Under the circumstances of constant, accidental manipulation, it's conceivable that it's done in response to the inability to hold oneself back from another personal breach of code, in which case the possibilities aren't cleanly split between awareness versus a lack thereof, but include one wherein the behavior is a sort of waking nightmare of a compulsion — a mountainous protrusion jutting forth on account of more deeply buried internal conflicts of interest.

Often it's so that the face of what's wrong in a given scenario is symptomatic of a more deeply entrenched matter — not necessarily a more deeply entrenched problem. Beyond a certain depth in the exploration of character, the roots of what appear from the surface to be an obtrusively lodged edifice unveil the thing as indispensably affixed, and one is choiceless but to back away in awe-filled observation of the mass in its full, glorious complexity. The more alien the subject, the more intense the revelation when one finally digs deep enough to find a space they consider their own home interwoven with its foundations.

6

DEPTH PERCEPTION

The only option when one's path becomes a rut, is to intentionally stray. The quality of a rut is such that one's sight is obstructed in proportion with its depth, and so there exists an inverse relationship between the importance of springing forth from it in any random direction, and the ease with which that can be done. If the walls are so high that the threat of fatally falling is the main risk involved with overcoming them, the rut is veritably interpretable as a prison — and one's prolonged presence in it is little more than suicide the long way round anyway. The reason the phrase "the high road" insinuates superiority, is decipherable in that the physical atmosphere of such a road is opposite to that of imprisonment. Atop a ridgeline everything is visible, the air is crisp, and serenity permeates the experience.

There's a twofold consideration in determining whether to ascend or descend; the view from within any trench can be ascertained, and requires little energy expenditure to behold; the view from a ridge cannot be guessed, and is difficult to attain — i.e., the path one takes is predicated on what kind of relationship one possesses with respect to predictability and difficulty. Notice how they flip as either is occupied, though — the predictability and ease with which a trench is entered quickly translates into strife and confusion if one should eventually like to exit. It insidiously takes advantage of one's faculties in exchange for what luxuries it provides. A ridgeline offers ease of movement and clarity to those who sacrifice what it takes to scale it.

Once one arrives at either, the perspective therein becomes the new neutral ground, since the possibility of ascent or descent is virtually always available — but it's interesting to note what would happen assuming one could continue in either direction without being asphyxiated or otherwise obliterated by descending into the bowels of Earth, or ascending into the sky. In both cases, the relationship between ascent and descent vanishes, but in extraordinarily different ways. In the former, all visibility is lost, and one is wholly encased in molten rock — whereas in the latter, the entire universe becomes visible, and one floats without strain through the boundless infinitude of space, as far as can be managed before encountering the gravity well of some nearby celestial object. Such observations are solely for the sake of amusement, however, since it's the insurmountable limitation of death which lends value to the experiences derived from the contrast between the two.

Often on the course to some set point at altitude, is the misunderstanding that the opposing experience of descent is necessary in recuperating sufficiently for one to continue climbing. For the sake of an efficient ascent, it should be noted that though rest from constant strain is irreplaceable, it's never undergone by reversing one's progress in any way. If one's inclination is not only to abandon all discipline come the week's end, but to undergo some overwhelming sensory gratification in addition, the implication is not that there's been adequate toil to warrant the indulgence — but that a more enticing summit would function as a superior objective. In addition, one creates substantial stress for themselves locked into a rhythm of gain and loss which indefinitely prevents their development of fresh upper limits.

On the contrary, that experience is readily applicable to the endeavor of ascending more worthy peaks on account of the manufactured strain. Not so much if the time spent in any one place is minimal, however, given it's just as hard on one to repeatedly rebound from a celebratory slide to the bottom without idling, as it would be to scale ceaselessly. In any event, the optimal way is to ascertain an adequate objective as early as possible, and recover without sacrificing territory on the approach by using time to assume a static position between stints of effortful movement.

As far as habituated sliding goes, its remediation should be undertaken with patient persistence. The unique obstacle included in this particular area is that for each time one harshly redresses themselves, the subsequent dismay unwittingly stokes the perpetuation of that error. The key is not in some self-righteous reprimand which places one's identity under irresolvable interrogation — it's in the strict, calm adherence to the intent of willfully molding the future, and capping credence for the past only insofar as there's usable information nestled in it.

Should moments come to pass where one toggles uncontrollably between the selection of what harms them and their desired direction, so be it — it's the psychological equivalent of one's core shaking as a beginner to planks. Once it passes, which, as everything else, it inevitably will, proceed peaceably — undaunted in the quiet aftermath. It may happen more times than can be counted, the critical aspect of the practice is to relish the dearth of restriction in the moments following the intermittent discomfort of the molting process. In time, the intervals between instances of self-contradictory behavior will widen until they're altogether forgotten. No child, once their growing pains subside, dwells on what suffering they went through to the degree that it stalls them in their pursuit of whatever they're oriented toward — the stress undergone in consequence to shifting one's sails can serve, once over, as both a trophy and a measuring stick in the righteous humiliation of what strife looms on the horizon.

One's relationship to time plays an enormous role in how effectively they'll be able to move. The attitude taken with respect to the fact that there's a scarcity of it is of primary importance, because the choice to fight or recede in response spells the difference in whether one can leverage it. The underlying importance of temporal constructs is that they constitute the most basic tiers of divisible energy. The amount of time at any given person's disposal scales one to one with their potential. To maintain the position under any circumstance that there's no need to rush, but become aroused when another downplays the importance of money, is like a pilot being concerned with their bird's paint job to the exclusion of the rate at which it's burning fuel. Not to suggest "rushing" is the most effective means of proceeding, as it disorients one's capacity to pay the requisite amount of attention necessary in legitimately maximizing economy — but the point stands that the monetary resources at one's disposal are secondary in their importance compared to time.

Prolonged exposure to whatever feelings inhibit one from using their time as fruitfully as possible holds the potential to transform them into enjoyable indications that one is on a suitable course. That is to say, in the moments preceding the first step into some commitment, the flitting anxiety which may normally trigger a drawn out dance with procrastination, can be reinterpreted as excitement — its presence the tense air prior to the beginning of a race. If one can habituate themselves to standing on their figurative starting blocks in that tension without walking off the track, the inaudible crack of an invisible pistol's blank tears through one's perception by virtue of their presence alone — one's latent energy cut loose in that instant, and movement therefrom transpiring nearly of its own accord. The intimation prior to that phantom percussion which would otherwise incite the departure of focus is borne of the wholly rational assessment that whatever unscathed hill one is meant to punch through will present itself as even more of a bitch once attended than it is just to stare at — but that's only so from however many yards away one stands. To break one's focus from the minuscule point of initial contact for that reason, is to succumb to the illusion that there's no hope to enter one's vehicle observed from a distance, because it's too small — i.e., to divorce oneself from the possibility of attainment by heeding an incompatibly disproportionate perspective.

For as typical an occurrence as this is, its insidiousness is concealed in that once accustomed to, the surrounding world transforms for one into a hopelessly impregnable fortress — the way in blocked for anything that might ameliorate one's aversion to new information, and helplessness pervading its interior ambiance as the exits seal. The act of deeming avenues of pursuit unviable is gradually incapacitating — akin in its progression to Lou Gehrig's disease. Without the faculty of defiant persistence, one will discard every other tool at their disposal useful for manageably positioning themselves relative to their obstacles — learning to attribute the impotence they've personally cultivated as endemic to everyone, and childish shortsightedness to the suggestion of sincere optimism and a thirst for adventure.

It's of course realistically feasible that the inverse is undergone — apparently harmless situations changing into extreme threats as one draws closer. The key in surpassing self-imposed limitations and increasingly tangible danger alike lies in one's maintenance of attention. The evolution, or lack thereof, of any phenomenon's refraction as it makes itself proximal to one's locus of perception, should never be used to construct a conceptually infallible trajectory in place of its primary observation — only what's parallel to oneself functionally submits to such projections, just as driving alongside a mountain range is the only scenario wherein there's a static roster of notability concerning it. Parallel relations are, however, exceedingly rare as far as the temporary ones — with the constant examples essentially imperceptible as separate from the self, because they'd kink in perfect proportion to one's distinct heading from birth to the grave.

For the most part one travels in an arbitrarily oblique fashion to everything beyond their nearest conceivable destination, which means there's something like a forty-five degree slice in front of each person with which it makes sense to do nothing save silently apprehend as it dances before them. There's a reason it's referred to as "talking shit" when one boasts of ground they've yet to take, and it translates both to the reason consistently arrogant individuals address entire domains of experience as opposed to those at a middle distance, and why buying insurance is a good idea — there's nothing more disruptively volatile than the forecast of the near future. Ascertaining the most functionally attended swath of data to the tight exclusion of excess is absolutely prerequisite to favorably covering ground. Otherwise, one's obtuse realm of concerns conforms their disposition into that of a prey animal — despite the anxious use of wide, depthless, monocular apprehension being largely wasted on the human organism.

Each exists on a unique precipice defined by the point past which patterns are no longer intelligibly perceptible. The reason is because the entirety of the familiar domain is characterized by some aspect of consistency — i.e., the categorically innocuous is constituted by what's predictable. Wisdom is conflated with calm because as patterns become apprehendable in the environment — the illusion of the perceiving individual's threat-tolerance is proportionately augmented in others' eyes therein.

It's referred to as an illusion because there's a constant balance on either side of the threshold past which things either begin making sense, or cease to. The ways of envisioning this, though both functionally arrive at the same conclusion — assume there's either an infinite amount of assimilable information, or a finite amount. The former is essentially the notion that the set of all problems, solved and unsolved alike, is boundless — just as the universe may be infinitely voluminous. A line drawn anywhere within such a space can serve as its center, and so whether or not it repositions relative to any local features is inconsequential with respect to the larger picture. If there's a finite quantity of problems, human beings are such that the world is only digestible through the opposition between pleasure and displeasure, and so whether to anybody else one's position includes lesser or greater amounts of either, since it's the individual's composition rendering their salience — they're always balanced the same way the sum of a quadrilateral's angles always equates to three-hundred-sixty degrees.

Not just the division between individuals, but the spectrum of desirability in its entirety — are most applicably dealt with as aesthetic matters. It may appear as though there would be a lack of clarity respecting the optimal path forward through this lens, which is accurate in that the attributed aesthetic value any could bestow a given subject is borne of too complex an amalgam of data points, unbound not only on the whole from common measure, but in specifics from communicable justification due to what ambiguous or spontaneous intuitions it may factor in — to the end of referential comparison. Doing so would sensitize one to the greater spectrum of aesthetic potential, but that simplifies to a dice roll as far as might be useful in fulfilling one's own.

The merit in aesthetic evaluation is as a scale which underpins one's entire selection of actionable schemes, delineating their viability not simply on the basis of

calculated rationality, instinct, or emotional appeal —
but with every available faculty simultaneously. To see
it as the case — consider that in no other domain save
for the arts, whose judgment is natively predicated on
aesthetic appeal, is criticism through every perspective
equally armed with the potential to validly influence the
field of opinions wherein some subject stands suspended.
Trivial as it may sound before the point past which
the arts are appreciable as subordinately nuanced only
to direct experience itself, the mutuality of their most
fitting style of appraisal therefrom seen — it's really no
wonder the attempt to cram one's whole life through *any*
finite quantity of evaluative apertures is insufficient for
personally experiencing alignment with one's most suitable
path.

It isn't necessarily as though such an alignment
would spell the elimination of tribulation, but the
friction borne of one's intentions in that event extricates
its disproportional presence from the internal or the
external, making it so what growth transpires on
either front occurs in tandem on its inverse — a
certain economy of energy thereby facilitated. Each front
being a functionally boundless territory, the expectation

that they'd be satisfactorily equilibrated with restricted measuring implements from either is something like hoping to construct an exhaustive architectural blueprint with a barometer and a couple of well-trained dogs.

The reason the arts stand as the nearest exemplification of life is because what constitutes art is definitionally unrestricted. That's not to suggest all art crosses every conceptual boundary, but it all at least holds the potential to — depending on who's doing the observing. Since all of it warrants the same stress-testing, so to speak — the lenses eliciting appreciation for certain pieces can be applied without inhibition in the examination of others one may not suppose they'd be generically exalted through. It's with this method cascades of uniquely personal relevance emerge from the mundane, its vast minutiae scintillating in accordance with one's varied implements of appreciation — distinctly illumined in their attention's light.

Should one find themselves on the receiving end of such a process — what's revealed is a previously undisclosed depth of meaning within. The sensation of another seeing something in oneself, though potentially pleasant — speaks primarily to the competence of the observer. To experience what's ordinary as possessed of innate richness is to carry that wealth within, though in exchange are proportional servings of filth and shit imbibed — its unfertilized propagation impossible. As far as what means whereby aesthetic value can be uncovered, it should be noted there's no domain wherefrom it's excluded, and so any attempt to establish hard boundaries beyond which the hunt for it is let alone — is in ignorance to the fact that the beast abides no fence.

The most comprehensive approach to unveiling it is to consciously subject oneself to what's unsettling about some certain situation despite the progressively increasing difficulty in doing so. The distance to the juncture where it blooms, and the temptation to risk its implosion, are negatively correlated. If one can hold themselves from surrendering to the anticipated satisfaction in its destruction, the trapped energy carries into previously unrelated spheres, emboldening their contents like cheese or wine charged with the depth of age, enlivening the gustatory satisfaction of what they complement to ends otherwise unrealistic. It's critical to acknowledge the power of restraint beyond both masochistic drudgery and hedonistic release — the perceptible domain is shallow and lacking with no patience to reveal the gradation present therein.

Though the recommendation is in consideration of unlocking what's essentially beauty from the environment — its increased density can prove exceptionally dangerous without the requisite degree of control. In lacking the ability to maintain a steady application of attention, what's lost is inconsequential each time one falters to some distraction than when there's a substantial accumulation of momentum eradicated in tandem with it. It's after the first successful experiments with the invocation of stillness under disconcerting conditions that what hard-fought gems one's acquired doing so can work against them — the registered threat of their loss instigating frenzy if they've been brought into the sphere of some hazard thereto too treacherous to infiltrate, to say nothing of what cataclysmic destabilization lurks on account of the heightened gratification promised in reintroducing the habit of releasing them.

Basically — if throwing one's bicycle down out of frustration becomes something appealing at speed on a motorcycle, there will be much bigger problems to sort out than whatever stimulus prompted the flirtation with that tantrum. Trusting in the process of what lead to one's grand new acquisitions is indispensable to holding a growth-oriented trajectory, which is why it's so imperative to consistently take strides to remind oneself how to tease the phenomenal from the detritus. It's tricky, because though some means is always at hand, it changes with the situation, and so cannot be mastered by way of mechanical repetition — as any finite process composite to the whole one seeks to establish cohesion with, might be. It's something like to make oneself as unobtrusive as possible while wading through what obfuscating waters mar the objective — such that some submerged causeway could reveal itself, not further disguised in the reverberations consequential to one's thrashing.

In releasing the pressure of finding the road to travel, it's shown — which makes quite a lot of sense, because why would anyone opt to spend their time anxiously beating their heels upon the surface of some infallibly prescribed, Ophanimically inscribed trail? It may be so that there is no way to go, and the prescription is just to shut up and relax until none appears so unsavory that any must be taken up with haughty airs of superiority, or dejected airs of the opposite. To make friends with the Labyrinth is to accept what gifts it has to impart — they are many, and varied.

There's an anxiety permeating the modern mind linked to two basic misunderstandings. The first is that feeling emotions is potentially lethal, and the second is that anything can be done about the gravity they present themselves with, without adding to it. Becoming frustrated with them because they offer no tangibly dignified course forward is like becoming frustrated with an exit sign for lacking any indications as to whether left or right is the best way to proceed once one's passed it — and refusing to do so in retaliation. Not only does the kicking and screaming in resistance to crossing the threshold they basically function as prevent the attainment of any perspective lending a hand up to where where one's just come from can be seen as necessarily left behind — but it's totally ineffective to any end at all. Once the limits are found within some bead on the line along which one follows as their way of life, it must be abandoned for the sake of finding the next one. Everything wanes this way — stumbling upon the new world and watching it crumble come hand in hand just as the thinning of a paint stroke at its end is signed up for on the glob's first contact with the respective substrate.

Conversely, fighting the turbulence involved in the penetration of some wondrous new sphere for fear of what sorrow lurks at its end is something akin to a miniature expression of suicide — the demolition of opportunity accepted as collateral in one's escape from agitation. There is no real escape, however, without taking on the full brunt of death, and so what transpires in place is merely a postponement of the saga in question. This type of congestion can stop one dead in place for the full length of life, as seen in dysfunctional elders who rave about the "golden days" of youth — scraping particulate matter from the bottom of their barrel of experience in stalwart refusal to endure *anything ever again*, staving off life as though doing so is anything less than a cheap death in disguise. This can go on indefinitely because no one has the right to impose how or when or why the past should be abandoned, only to watch as one's identity is dragged through muddy gravel as the present moment tows them mercilessly through the years, until the sweet release they should have given themselves is finally dropped like an anvil forged from the combined pity of all the sky's angels, sighs of relief and prayers for peace found — released from those fond of them.

7

BY ALL MEANS ONWARD

Intent only manifests in response to the impediment of otherwise unconscious processes. Everything that runs smoothly is fundamentally involuntary; one's heartbeat, the rhythm of air visiting and departing one's lungs, the countless parts cohesively functioning in a motor vehicle — all indisputably unproblematic background phenomena until interrupted. Insinuated from this is not only that death and perfection are one and the same state, but that all desire to live irresolvably represents a certain longing for discordance.

That being said, the emergence of life is not something voluntarily undergone — and so there's an interesting margin between suicide and interference where the experience of being alive occupies the same set encircling the inscrutably impeccable; clouds, cats, fire, mountains, babies, the way opaque liquids slowly coalesce with transparent ones when poured, etc. It's an elusive task to establish the conditions wherein human beings lose this quality, however, because the dividing slider can be cogently placed beyond the point where bloody conflict is as functionally determinate as planetary orbit, or before the point where dressing oneself is a matter of personal responsibility — the ineffability of perfection makes it a matter of sprinting on ice in unbroken dress shoes to contrive the optimal system of personal organization, just as the infinite distance from zero to one cannot be crossed using a solitary rational number between them.

The process of establishing a phenomenal pattern could be said to transpire as a result of one's commitment to locating the boundary past which they no longer possess control — like an increasingly ridiculous game of fetch one plays with themselves. This is based on the observation that the aforelisted phenomena interface with the world at the very limit of what they can manage — those inanimate examples manifest in flush accordance with the physical laws, existing in states of maximum tension in that any amount of destruction they undergo definitively changes *what they are.* In other words, they qualify as spectacles because they incontrovertibly operate on the brink of their own cessation one-hundred percent of the time. The animate examples are similar — they're constantly snug against the upper bounds of their own intelligence, imbued with a certain aspect of grace for their inability to withhold themselves from maximal expression.

Though such splendor is observable in other human beings, it may be in its essence incapable of flourishing in the confines of self-consciousness. In what moments could personally be described *and* corroborated as instances of this variety — it's standard for one to describe their display with a striking absence of recollective efficacy, almost as though they weren't present. In smaller-scale emergences; the way one walks, or looks, or what elegance they possess in their mannerisms or in some modicum of personal conduct — ever-present is the intimation that they're unaware of what's illuminated about them.

The grand irony in this is that each consciously strives to embody the aspect being discussed, but it slips between the fingers in a sort of mercurial recalcitrance come the concrescence of its naked observation, and one's fusion with it. The anxiety accompanying the event of one's fading perceptual grasp, then, may be symptomatic of that nakedness being taken up — its characteristic vulnerability therefrom personally assimilated in exchange for office as the thing itself. Once involved with the next stage of evolution, turning back wherefrom one sprung with hopes of invoking the chrysalis' sacred protection appears disturbing in the same sense it would to coddle and pet one's dead dog. Once the old house, habit, relationship, etc. starts to look stiff with rigor mortus despite what attachments remain, the sad reality is that it had been replaced with an idea sometime before it died — its curtain having fallen before a distracted audience, the funerary preparations neglected. One finds themselves forced from such a point to proceed regardless — a planet's worth of sentiment is inadequate to pull off a resurrection.

If the idea of forward movement appears too absurd to carry out, the capacity to reduce the size of one's steps becomes literally more important than having legs. The experience of fulfillment that incentivizes momentum's accumulation must be undergone on a regular enough basis to justify the energy expenditure, and if the tools at one's disposal are insufficient to hit those milestones, the pride involved in determining their distance needs to be remorselessly deserted that they might draw closer and multiply until manageably attained. An enormous sticking point respecting one's ability to conduct themselves as such is the willingness to be perceived as a failure in lieu of a liar.

Those giving chase to the allure of lionhearted legends who call their shots and either make them or go out having "tried their best," are prone to paint a minor tire puncture as the shattered final front at Thermopylae. Boasting of what accomplishments lie on the horizon is almost never functional to the end of shortening one's distance to them, and if caught between the ever-growing lack of realism in one's verbalized predictions, and the shame of their betrayal in favor of a more functional agenda — silently renovating the timeline one elects to regard beats the hell out of the alternative just the same as disemboweling an assailant with a letter opener beats the hell out of trying to land a shot between their eyes with an unreadied rifle at half a meter. If the target is not the conscious priority, it can be counted on to slip beyond one's realm of focus as reliably as the road ahead in the event of a prolonged gander at what scenery lies past its shoulder — be it constituent to the final destination, or not.

The mind's tendrils elongate immeasurably far past any common bounds that might normally pose themselves as manditorily observed should one opt to uncinch their expectations of what context will accompany their accomplishments — i.e., one isn't genuinely fighting unless they're fighting dirty. If they threaten to present no subsequent obstacles, inhibitions regarding favorably boding means should be treated as parasitic. In addition to opening avenues through which one might single out superior angles of engagement, with practice — one situates themselves in line with their vision for the future more efficiently on account of their willingness to tolerate imperfect circumstances. It's frequently the case that mechanics are borne of children who find themselves obliged to fix what they've broken in the thralls of their explorative curiosity, and the messiness endemic to that particular process of development isn't of negligible relevance to the consistency with which it churns out career tradespeople.

Becoming frustrated with the fact that a minimal quantity of misalignment must be swallowed on the way to consistently striking one's desired outcome is like becoming frustrated with the walls for not bearing one's desired hue before having made an effort to paint them. Dissatisfaction is an irreplaceable fuel source for invoking one's desired changes, but it's poisonous if left unattended in the same way as an aimlessly hyperactive toddler; both contain the possibility to yield marvelous things with the requisite application, and equally, otherwise, to raze what environments might be leveraged to nurture them. There are two ways to adequately manage dissatisfaction — the first is to cognitively recontextualize its origin as beneficial, and the second is to shed it following a successful confrontation with its cause. Both methods can be honed independently, as well as applied in tandem.

The former, though not typically thought of as such — is most accurately denoted the *skill* of gratitude. The most common perspective respecting gratitude is as a thing emerging organically in the ambiance of those circumstances which would rightfully invoke it — which is true in the same sense that running is a thing which will commence without any personal governance in events triggering flight responses. Instinctual engagement with either are best considered introductory — far cries from the enormous technicality with which their mastery necessitates familiarization. In one for whom gratitude is foundational to operating, their stride possesses remarkable consistency through otherwise irreconcilable settings as far as their standard effect on morale, because one manages to sift the whole universe into the subcategories of good experiences and good lessons — never finding themselves in an unlubricated position to enact their will. On the other hand, one qualmless with the notion of testing themselves outright against what static they encounter takes the form of a skilled knight — a sharp habit of dispatching bestial adversity at hand to keep disappointment at bay. Unprejudiced with how their might might be wielded, they strip without hesitation the skins in their vicinity potentially useful as defensive leathers, rather than circumventing treacherous paths strewn before them.

Though the means are posed as interchangeable, and it would be in error to assert the contrary, they're often mutually limited — the cultivation of either postponed at the behest of the other's, initiating a certain pattern of neglect; spiritual discipline is frequently spurred from the detritus of great physical or familial calamity, where no power or influence holds sway to close the imperceptible wounds; one may forge for themselves a steel work ethic or cold analytical capacity resultant of an impractically sensitive or idealistic upbringing, lauding competence in the external world tantamount to the Platonic ideal of security. It's unnecessary to pass judgment on one making use of either, because clarity is a thing voluntarily sacrificed in exchange for the amelioration of yearning — a thirst none go indefinitely without slaking.

As far as problems go, deeper solutions breed superior reinforcement in the systems they arise in — but they never quit going. It's a valuable practice to hold oneself from interfering with that emptiness gouged by acute longing, because it aids perception in every sense; pinpointing a sound is simplest in silence, an object in open space, and a thought where others pose no clutter. One might only be reasonably measured relative to the depths at which they'd motionlessly gaze.

It's safe to reason the optimal balance of gratitude and competence is basically whatever appears at hand to one's closest approximation of their personal apotheosis, since it's always some steps ahead, and thus possessed of either in superior density to what's available in one's current inventory. Though bound to change with time, that vision calls one forth toward itself to reveal what prospective growth couldn't be considered from a place preceding its encounter. The physical and emotional development taking place en route serve to unbind one's volition from their maximal thresholds — progressively setting one free from the imprisoning cordage of distress.

8

GNOSTIC TEMPERANCE

What is the significance of a coincidence? It's something like a small jewel whose potential is either nonexistent, or usefully relevant, depending on the witness' shifting predilection — a kind of perpetually uncollapsed "Schrödinger's meaning" of a phenomenon, who'll just as readily serve to bolster a hypothesis as fade, pointless, into the background static of necessarily inadmissible qualia. What's marked about a coincidence is it's tainted with a uniquely personal quality, forcing one to abide the implication that they themselves are somehow inextricably involved with what inscrutable series of events proceeds both to and from it — should they resolve it warrants attention. It's clear who's heeding a narrative constructed from coincidence to coincidence, because they'll appear as in the midst of an invisible adventure.

Eventually the word "coincidence" becomes like the word "mound" to one who has exalted some set to the status of a mountain — fostering much confusion and division in that cavernous ravine between *them*, and the like who've snuffed it outright from the subset of what deserves acknowledgment. Understandable as it is to disregard the thing for being superstitious and irrational given its basically nonexistent, or at the very least dubiously communicable, wake and trajectory — the question's begged of whether as an abstraction it couldn't be of some justified utility. To go so far as to impose the conjured implications of some perceived series of synchronicities, on others, in cases can feasibly grant one tangible influence, and though there's certain ethical contention concerning such behavior — that vanishes while what personal effect it provides persists, in the privacy of one's own psychology. Is there danger in taking silent sips of satisfaction in regular observation of the curiously unlikely?

It's nearly like asking the same of recreational drugs. For those in stark opposition, there's little that's convincingly acceptable about using what might be termed deliberately glorified confirmation bias to any end at all — the same way any deviation from what routine chemicals internally circulate in one's body might be regarded nothing but worrisome. To draw the parallel deeper — the personal right to dictate what chemicals permeate one's bloodstream, and also the proposition that there's an inescapable baseline of dictation regarding it with every action one takes, both translate seamlessly into the coincidence question. The first is merely the assertion of "no harm no foul" — the right to imbibe drink or attribute importance to mysterious happenstance needn't be meddled with insofar as what resultant destruction transpires extends no further than the individual's property. The second is more interesting — because there's an approximate range between coffee and diphenhydramine wherein the physiological repercussions stretch from insomnia all the way to insanity and death, but their use hardly escapes into the dimension of indefensibility in common discourse.

Even below that — the human organism is deconstructible into the periodic table, and so not only is every qualitative assessment it's possible to make of someone an evaluation of chemicals, but likewise expressed *as* a dynamic amalgam of them. There's the mirror image of socially manageable assertions about synchronicity, spanning from harmlessly noting a song's seeming description of personal circumstance, debatably right up to the whole edifice of astrology. The deconstruction of the word "coincidence" yields a second, though not mutually exclusive meaning to that currently regarded; any number of things occupying the same space — a definition which fits the entirety of the universe quite comfortably within it. At the end of the day, then, for the strictest materialists and the most dispositionally aqueous metaphysicists alike — what is, is a chemical coincidence.

Isolating the place between meaningless events and those it's critical to attend traces clean around the mysteriously coincidental, much the same way jewelry is bordered flush on its ends by functionality and uselessness — classlessness regarding either made clear when attention's drawn to them with a shamelessly heavy hand, but also when dismissed outright. Perhaps it's cheating to shoot between what edges of anything constitute the juncture delineating the appropriate time and place for it, using the quite universal characteristic of finite contextual adequacy as a means of making comparisons — but it's basically evident that what's affecting in a given comparison relies on the similarity established between disparate subjects, and the contrast teased from those nearly indistinguishable. That in mind, perhaps there's hardly more artful an execution than to paint the immaterial, and the metals gouged from the Earth's crust to the end of carnal adornment, a common hue.

As far as bad omens — to associate or concern oneself with them is functionally equivalent to the deliberate consumption of bleach. It might be argued that from a perspective indiscriminately delighting in the ascription of positivity to what causally cryptic signs arise — the tendency toward the opposite may also be pronounced. Though shortsighted to take it as granted, that pitfall may be rationally considered at least in the vicinity of such a one, and tripped into by members of the subclass lacking a nuanced appreciation for what extent of influence one renders themselves vulnerable to in the divorce of meaning from logically authenticatable origins. A directionless foray into the mystical realm of universally calculated serendipity is quite enough to extricate oneself from the eerily permeable veil of societal sanity upheld in the struggle for reason — it's not without cause flagrant naïveté with respect to this is apt to incite distaste.

It's interesting to see at what point arguments cease to appear valid across the spectrum of individuals, or the variety in where existential bedrock is propounded to exist, given it's frequently described at coordinates others might regard as on the way to, far past the point, or nowhere relative to where one is personally confident it is. Any combination of habit and veneration can be — from uninhibited spending and stalwart conservatism, to promiscuity and Catholicism, to say nothing of the stereotypical and completely uninferable attitudes corresponding to the second object of each of those examples. Pacifists may gush over their infallible love of Christ and His boundless reciprocity, unfazed their dogma shares a litter with the likes of crusaders and inquisitors. Those positing the colossal merit of rationalism may make no mention of, or alternatively dismiss the irony in that the notion of nature's conquest through number and measure was incepted by, by Descartes' own description, an angel who visited him in his dreams.

In one sense it's nice that no perspective is incontrovertibly annihilated by the presence of any other, each free to find comfort in whichever pleases them — but in another it's terrifying and disturbing that any demonstrable consensus in this matter is certifiably mythological, almost as though the truth of the situation is revealed merely insofar as it prompts any to find some abysmal minimum of semantic stability concerning life on Earth, and absolutely no more. Intimations that significance is baited from invisible, ever-retracting fingertips affixed to incomprehensibly ascendant creatures writhing in fits of interdimensional jocularity flicker as what's corroborably endured in those pockets of frustrated perplexity, which is why it's indispensable to hold a hand over the plug lending power to what intellectual components could otherwise rip the psyche apart with unbridled centrifugal momentum in enabling the retaliatory pursuit of what always turns out to be one's own tail.

Often that effort to quell the cascade of anxious questioning preventing one from functioning fluidly is juxtaposed in its effect with precisely what it's employed to replace, much the same way an addict will falter in becoming rid of their pet vice without occupying themselves with some partial reflection of it.

Reasoning, as a means, is perhaps that most vulnerable to becoming corrupted by pathological concern. Any given distraction is always a potentially loaded crack pipe for one basically incapable of piloting their temperament. Whether it's feasible to convey the habitual impediment of redlining one's mental faculties an individually combatable craving is more or less an extension of the controversial discussion surrounding the moral vs. disease models of addiction, because to the degree the behavior is considered involuntarily afflictive, no supposition of voluntary remediation can be regarded operable.

As potentially insensitive as it is to color any kind of pathology operator error, the domain of conscious attention lands alarmingly far behind the point described in the previous chapter where getting dressed in the morning is something under the jurisdiction of personal control, which is half the reason there's so much resistance to the inclination toward alleviating the responsibility of its domestication from the individual. The other half has to do with the fact that the proclivity for outsourcing solutions would effectively extend into the root of what a person *is* — because as no more than a fleshy composite of receptors at the environment's unremitted mercy, the notion of intent itself, paradoxically, is eradicated in the course of its incessant gratification. As an individual — volition is a vital instrument; as an uncomfortable amalgam of nerves requiring constant amelioration — volition is barely more than a wart forestalling one's application as a battery. To fly blind to the iota of predation in that which would offer itself a welcome place to indefinitely rest is just as foolish as to ignore what benefit principally resides in anything stimulating stress. There's a leap required to measure a phenomenon in the light of its opposite portent, but once done — what merit lies in its engagement reveals itself more roundly. For example — in the way a day at the beach is most suitably enjoyed with a cognizance of sunburns, and a strenuous exercise most functionally undergone with an appreciation for the growth it facilitates.

The concern of somehow winding up backwards through whatever counterintuitive evaluative approaches come to mind in response to this notion, is offset precisely by the implications proceeding from the fact that they arise instinctively. The expectation evoked by any given scenario can optionally clue one into what inverse perspective the blind spots they're possibly harboring would likely be found in — a minimum standard of vigilance in acknowledging this is not sufficient to capsize one's entire identity, and hones the discriminatory precision useful for lubricated maneuver through the gargantuan, intricate matrix of perceptual nodes to which threads of communally apprehendable meaning beckon to be lashed.

9

TO UNVEIL PRESSURE

Plans are designed to frighten oneself into compliance with one's own intentions, their edges representing the frontier past which the unknown reigns, whose wilds would be nightmarish to roam with only the tools one possesses sans the companionship of a learned cartographer — as in a mentor, or a leader. Getting in touch with the raw horror intrinsic to the threat of an untimely death, and by extension a meritless life, is not only damn near more important than staying hydrated (otherwise to what end does one persist?), but imbues the present moment with the kind of value lending credence to a plan's implementation — to be deleted by a stray bullet while quibbling frustratedly with the ultimately trivial is not something intelligently left to chance. Not that life's meaning need be laid plain in invincibly distinguishable terms, but in any case no dearth of direction resides in tandem with those whose margins surrounding their proficient familiarization with purpose share a domain with the failure to survive.

Fretting over one's relative stability in response to that notion is something like standing agape with envy at others charging headlong into the fires of battle with sticks for possessing such indomitable vitality — with a long-sword of expertly refined steel in hand. Passively excusing oneself for idling ensconced out of touch with the physiological pressures of what's tense betwixt inconsolably gnashing teeth and the tantalizing scuttling of its own next meal, is delusional cowardice — like an officer behind front lines shielding their inner eye from visions of a possible future where they're the ones exchanging lead. Arguably, such behavior tempts that reality closer.

The gravity of this pending rectification needn't be responded to with some dramatic overture — that'd be tasteless. A stoic inventory of time and resources is all that's necessary, the former the pressure and the mold for the latter's application. Considering what breadth a human being's hedonic set point can dance about in the course of one's experience is really the only thing demanding appreciation to the end of christening what ground one stands on as adequately proceeded from. What's fucked up about being made to journey forth into a preemptively failed endeavor is exactly the same thing as what makes it enjoyable. Imagine samurai awaking each morning thrilled to coexist with another sunrise, salaciously anticipating violence with the full awareness that the katana branding them, whether they're freshly bathed and in dyed robes sat astride a steed bequeathed by some wealthy feudal lord, or masterless, filthy, and on foot walking down dusty roads in war-torn and lawless countryside — rendered it such that their final moments of inevitable evisceration lurked unavoidably behind every cluster of foliage, whispered its irrepressibility from just past each threshold, and made itself known in the gazes of the innocent, the animals, and the elderly, so that no step taken could be without salience, no interaction without significance, and nothing committed to without the absolute maximal vehemence of life behind it.

To say one should live as though they're smoking their last day as spoken to doesn't quite function to highlight what requires attention — the acknowledgment that it's constantly a potential reality, does. There's a fine line between putting on airs of fatalism and a regard for what's actually the situation, but since one's own death hovers like a specter outside the window a perpetual abstraction, it's harder to lend unadulterated focus than what's as concrete as a mug or a cicada or a telephone pole. What's tangible binds focus by virtue of its presence, and so naturally since nothing about being a corpse really provides a perceptual foothold, it's considerably more elusive. There's a range between the inevitably undergone and the purely conceptual, with death the only thing truly being both — but just because there's no point of reference for how to treat it doesn't mean it should be assimilated into either corner exclusively.

The revulsion generated in the witness of something dead instigates a spiritual equivalent of granular convection — rendering conspicuous the greatest constituents of one's total set of concerns. Carrying what's most massive at the forefront of perception makes one vulnerable the same way one might feel to publicly tote around the priciest articles of their domicile. Feeling the full weight of that importance, each move reverberates with the existentially titillating prospect of its exposure to influence — a gross increase in sensitivity thereby undergone. There's a certain logic in the avoidance of this exercise because it's indisputably unpleasant, but what's neglected with such reasoning is the appreciation that life's total advance in resolution would provide the detailed immersion seeing one celebrate an unavoidable stray bullet as a worthy culmination.

The prospective tsunami of death gains an inch for everyone renouncing life in favor of the numb soullessness of a husk's lot, passing the buck to those who'd bleed to fortify the dikes. The world has a funny, albeit ominous way of granting wishes. Rich or poor, old or young, calls for death in jest in place of sighs in stride to win the day make for the perfect kind of slow drip apathy which invites destruction as reliably as sarcasm over text invites sincere responses. The comfort involved with composting effortful involvement and opting instead to make like a cadaver as a means of coasting by is to gamble between turning oneself into one of two things — a parasite, or a parasite and a time-bomb. Parasite because endeavoring to do things one would only barely rather do than die places a remarkably low ceiling on the efficacy they can harness engaged in it, and time-bomb because if and when the combined contribution (rather lack-thereof) of so many purposeless and destitute, crests the tipping-point toward catastrophic instability, they'll evaporate under the pressure of their own incompetence with a front that what poisonous passivity brought it about in the first place was wholly separate from themselves.

The trick with combating such a gloomy proposition is not to exhaust oneself in any indignant outpour of vitriol, but to confine the resultant energy such that it works to germinate throughout what of the world one rightly possesses dominion over. Entertaining the pursuit of extinguishing contention under the pretense of justifiable vilification not only saps the energy otherwise useful as creative fuel for the development of one's ideal ambiance, but serves to stoke that contention further. Consider that a deliberately summoned flame, whether candle or campfire, responds to the purposeful application of one's breath in a way which works favorably — whether quelled or tended. Should a fire be large enough and fearsome enough that it *arrests* one's attention, the same way one finds themselves perturbed by unignorable signs of societal decay — little can be done as a solitary agent that won't aerate it propagatively.

The blessing of such an impasse is that if one can muster the resolve to face that flame with a healthy respect for what it is — it can be trusted to indiscriminately burn everything aside from what one cannot be without. The contents of the small remaining sack one scrambles to collect from the ablaze maze of picture frames, sentiments, and comforts, are forcibly unveiled through that blistering scavenge as most densely potentiated among one's accumulations for making what one will of themselves in their mastery of the subsequently negotiated ashen hellscape, and thereafter the establishment of something with durability superior to that which was lost. Preemptively and efficiently should this be done before that caliber of chaos is reached, but it's so that the only relevant discipline possible to call forth is proportional with the degree to which one appreciates the risk of being razed as such — hollow motivation scrounged beyond the sector of outright unacceptable personal risk to the end of anything more than insipid, milquetoast steps forth, is fruitless to the human spirit; the false flora cultivable from that vapid soil devoid of angst, hate, loss, fear, and despair, cannot be used invigoratively. The proposition that such feelings have no place in the human endeavor is like arguing the uselessness of wind to a mushroom spore.

If inspiration paints the end, frustration provides the traction for moving one toward it. The common denominator among all the feelings rendered basically villainous is the raw energy possessed within them. To alienate one's conception of self from the hurt and the enraged is to force their expression from the fossilized scaffolding of lethally primal tantrums — that which calls one to scream and tear and disembowel and violate requires the imposition of structure to guide it if it's to be leveraged prior to outright disaster, but that structure's construction is impossible without the common exaltation of primordially violent energy, and the willingness to honor its inextricable value. It is far from feasible to train a dog before gaining its trust.

Neglecting to wade through one's own filth on account of fear is to leave that responsibility for whoever's unlucky enough to find themselves skewered between the full brunt of its discovery and a hard place. Forget the momentary cost of its review — none deserve to be crushed beneath a waterfall of fuckery solely because the dam withholding one's emotions was too long in the charge of any outside the blast radius of its potential malfunction. One can't lift a finger before admitting to themselves the management of their emotional quality is something for which no other should be held accountable. For as high and as daunting as the waves in oneself appear, the unceasing drive to tame them ought to shape one's decisions.

There is a stark difference in consequence between aiming to fix one's problems, versus to distract oneself from them. Though in the course of their resolution there may be pain and angst, knuckles split and tears shed for how abominably every nuance of uncensored reality oppressively drags its split and infected nails through the vulnerable flesh of one's sanity — in hiding from them, one's course forth is sailed in forfeit to indispensable reinforcement. Staving off irritation is one thing, but to do so by means which circumvent that worthy road one selects for themselves is to throw down an empty rifle instead of reloading it under the threat of an oncoming volley.

It's often the case that what's comforting becomes confused with that slew of activities one partakes in which make them feel incompetent, but failing to discriminate these from one another lodges one in so narrow a window through which they can conscionably act that disproportionately more time will be spent in anxious lamentation than selectively defending against what poses legitimate impediment.

10

A FESTIVAL OF SEX AND DEATH

The present moment being a thing possessing both what's newest and what's oldest, it's possible to look at the world as primarily either. Neither is more real than the other, so to rise each morning disdainful of the droning monotony of another day in the litany of endless days, thrilled to absorb the fresh complexity of the clouds' crimson soaked edges as the sun splays lazily up from the horizon, pleased to awaken in a comfortable rhythm of predictability, or terrified for what new and unknown horrors may lurk in the coming hours — flow with one another just as seamlessly as water through a brook. In light of this apparent paradox, it becomes quite justifiable to sprint in the direction of any particular age-related implication. There are those who see the rapid advances in society and technology as the dermic cracking and wrinkling of a thing approaching its end — that end has been nigh for as long as anyone can remember. There are those who see nothing but the unbearably dense potential for the situation's rapid evolution — a promise that's been loaded for as long as anyone can remember.

As incompatible as they might sound on the surface, it makes perfect sense that a place notable for its mass of shifting cycles wouldn't yield on close analysis as merely characteristic of one section of one. It's said beyond the constraints of the third dimension an entity would see a thing at a glance in the totality of its temporal expression. Humans are caught between the finite stimuli coloring their momentary sensations and their intimations of the eternal just as surely as they're caught between the Earth and the sky; denizens of the cosmically intertidal — gyrating inconsolably at the precipice of causality. Fascinatingly, thoughts retain the possibility of generating untold quantities of friction should one repeatedly vacillate in interpreting their potential origins as basically oppositional to each other.

Since the common standard of mental and emotional quality appears to be a passively managed lull peppered with intermittent peaks of mania — any attempt to retool its baseline meets with a hard-fought trek through what status quo cultural suppositions anchor it beneath the surface above which its rhythms might coincide with some semblance of desirability. Isolated experimentation will reveal what reasoning underlies a perspective is unbound from exclusive adherence to any particular narrative, but the thick anxiety associated with the indeterminacy of such semantic limbo, and particularly the tension related to maintaining it while conscious of one's presence in a group — more often than not sees one's disposition fall in line with that of the masses. To peel oneself away from the tendency to minimize the organic discriminatory processes permitting a utilitarian selection of thoughts, is to surgically extricate the notion that a potential mismatch in perspectives, internally or socially, is somehow intrinsically dangerous. Learning to cordially regard the coexistence of what innumerable possibilities lie before oneself is something akin to making available all the eighty-eight keys of a piano.

The capacity to cognitively manipulate some situation to one's advantage is hardly arcane. Virtually everything it's possible to look at comes in two flavors; spontaneous benign emergence, and tool in the figurative hand of one or many insatiably conniving creatures. The entirety of the latter category *is* the lens through which the most innocent beings conceivable justify the tearing asunder and the swallowing whole of what organic matter might perpetuate themselves; a willingness to mercilessly wring every vitalizing chemical one can from anything and everything is the absolute lowest tier buy-in for being allowed to participate in existence — to color the situation differently would be grossly misrepresentative.

That minimum standard of mutilation is welded irreversibly to the creative process, their ancient tango so pervasive, each facet of the human world can be walked back to its respective infancy in the mind of the individual who conceived it — the sprawling edifice interlaced with the writhing substructure of its own maternity ward, its progenitors snacking fervently on chicken nuggets as artfully crafted to evade sensory detection as having anything to do with billions of obliterated chickens as the infrastructure facilitating their delivery is to efficiently and affordably fuel all who gratefully partake. The same way it's a counterintuitive clusterfuck to deliberately locate the point of stability inside a running drying machine, is it to definitively pinpoint what part of the human organism, and by extension the enterprises consequential to it — adequately represent the body of their worth. The continual dance of all these things makes it such that any solitary assessment of their value based on criteria beyond the degree to which they functionally lend momentum to some other process, falls flat like an interjection intended to distill what's been said in the course of a conversation to some insoluble, i.e., closed-ended, conclusion.

A system is only exalted if in the course toward its exhaustion, enough energy is generated to facilitate a sum of tangential growth outweighing what it itself consumed throughout the course of its development. To be fulfilled is to witness one's literal and/or figurative progeny leap forth, fueled by one's own energy, to horizons unattainable in one's own time. It's illusory that boundless joy can be found in the generic picture of personal gratification not because there's some mysterious, carnally impenetrable firmament past which an infinitude of Earthly pleasures lie in wait postmortem — but because the bounds of personal identity simply need not yield to those of the flesh, or the team, or the country, or the planet.

There's a constant, limitless outward projection of aspiration in forms of life so rudimentary they aren't even biologically considered as such — as in the case of viruses. The retaliation to even the most minor suggestion that it be stifled is so strong and so immediate — that nucleus of unslakable augmentation automatically becomes the epitome of violence, or retreat, and discriminates against *nothing,* including its own appendages, to the end of bursting forth. One will wind up dead or abandoned so fast in the attempt to cram a lid on the expansion of life — not a singular bat out of hell could outpace the corresponding destruction. Markedly, the beauty in the expansion peaks in the moments its frontier is translated to a shiny new external vessel. Life as such is meant to continually make the miraculous pass-off over the void, because otherwise that abyssal rot germinates in those stagnant arterial corridors touched by time, who merely then entomb the dynamic vigor which once drove corporeal animation, in a quite avoidably final episode of vivisepulture.

This is a hard to shake drama to have painted — in a finite section of time where there is a delineable beginning and end, there's a narrative whose synopsis could unfailingly include the phrase

"striving in the face of..." This quip is ubiquitously descriptive of virtually every instant. It should never be neglected, however, that though the present is something generally conceived as in perpetual suspension between some representation of a beginning, whether the birth of the planet, one's newborn, oneself, the big move across the country or the world so long ago, or even just yesterday, or "just now," and some anticipated finality in what's called the future — the only actual experience is

The cool thing about the world is that it's perceptually permeable on every front. There isn't a single thing if attended intently enough that won't bloom into an orifice suitably large to facilitate exploration — which means, in effect, that anything imposing itself as a barrier can be laughed at and proceeded in spite of. Now that happens to *include* oneself, so there's no trivial amount of associated danger — but on the whole there are way more flying blind to the full extent of their unobtrusive, mortally inconsequential influence, than need weigh it against the destructive turbulence of its own recoil.

Perhaps the dearth of that permeability's exploitation has to do with the intimation that to move through the world as such is to subject oneself to some exceedingly distasteful rhythm of consumption and expulsion, as though taking advantage of opportunities to penetrate what stands before one is to become grotesquely involved with it as one might in passing through the torso of a dragon with a sword — or jungle, densely populated with nightmarish flora and fauna, with a machete. The trick to navigating what amount of change before oneself does not seem feasibly digested is to hash out to what degree one's current situation is coherently understood as reflective of the predicament being fixated on.

What irreducible mutability functions as the foundation upon which things manifest makes it such that that basic quality of shifting instability nascent before one can be robbed of its threatening airs through a thorough enough attendance to one's current condition — the entire field of possibility rendered indistinguishable from the ground one presently resides on. The scrambling specter depends on one's refusal to unveil it in order to maintain its presence. Just as any ghost remains inside a closet or beneath the stairs, its power flourishing insofar as there's the interval before its direct apprehension — so too are there ghosts in time, parading their threats just so long as one's none the wiser they're vulnerable and within reach. They develop fungally, feeding in those shadows untouched by actionable intention. They encroach for as long as the matter of their expulsion is postponed — then inevitably, slowly, one's deliberate ignorance nurtures them till they've the space on the back of one's neck for an abode, one's will crippled as the price for never having deigned to look them in the face.

It's not fallacious to argue humans are only atop the food chain on account of their advanced affinity for estimation, but it would be to claim that function divorced in its utility exclusive to the concerns of the present moment. Rarely is the maximum effective range of a thing a boundary against which it's reasonable to dwell. Prerequisite to the intellect's effective use is not only a standard of precision, only calculable and subsequently cultivable tested at some range relevant to oneself — but one of accuracy, that there's a tangible function in its particular orientation. As a creature inherently sensitive to gain and loss, it's not as though what merit in thought is unbound from thought's every subtlety, but the scattered mess of vaguely coherent points arising resultant of the thinker confounding their aiming faculty with the thoughts themselves, saps them of otherwise colossal power, and weakens them to possession by fruitless disquiet.

What's past the edge of reason does not eradicate the primary experience of being the same way it does one's conceptions. Consciousness apparently requires no minimum of intelligibility in its environment in order to persist. In fact, it may be the case that the most minuscule modicum of consciousness is functionally such that the extent of its experience is that to which it detects the possibility of coherence, but not coherence as such.

Though the generic course of an organism might be to gradually broaden its perception relative to what it's managed to familiarize itself with, the expanse of that radius can work against it should one encounter an anomaly on the frontier provoking a forced alteration in its greatest index of abstractions — resulting in the rapid internal proliferation of a kind of malignant bewilderment.

The same flavor of massively riveting fault pervading the psychic geography of Italy following Galileo's splash is merely a macrocosmic example of what can happen at the level of the individual should one accidentally manage to pry the panels labeled "obvious" off what unspeakable guts constitute the incorrigibly amorphous undercurrent upon which meaning makes do. A glance at the contents of human production reveals the lot predicated on the endeavor of pulling things together — grouping what of the world can be physically and conceptually tamed into replicable, non-divergent formulas useful for propagating the outward crystallization of indeterminacy into order.

The chaos, however, hides within the domesticated matters. As though they're coated in an iridescent film reflecting alternate hues to each — what duplicity of significance rears its head when a thing two or more familiar with in two or more ways becomes the subject of mutual attention can instantaneously incite an alarming interpersonal impasse if handled without a basic appreciation for the fact that a rock to one may be virtually anything to another. As when someone dies and their kin find themselves revealing their cards to one another respecting what suppositions they hold of the deceased; so unassailable is the basis around which earnest attempts at communicable apprehension slip that it's the calcified conglomerate of those exchanged feelings functioning to replace the person as a feature of the living world once they're gone. Loss is only palpable to the degree it affects what's left behind, and since nothing touches anything quite the same, it's less as though something definite vanishes, and more like the additional quality of absence is interpolated into its repertoire for every unique system with which it's affiliated.

In all that's mutually appreciable there are hard lines necessarily drawn past which intent discussion absolutely cannot go without dissolving the sanctity of the matter at hand; the rate at which caustic peculiarity leaks into some inner sanctum is negatively correlated with its seamless simultaneous conceptual renovation in the minds of all stakeholding parties. It's why what institutions lauded as timeless face onslaughts of backlash during attempts to shift with the age. Upending rupture consequential to the movement of any ancient object around which much has grown is seldom bargained for.

Despite what fragility those deeply entrenched in tradition subject their hearts to in refusing its exposure to anything outside the virtuous crawlspace within which they nervously prostrate themselves to dilapidated shrines to safety — there is hefty merit in a minimum of ritual. In its most rudimentary form, the value of performing an arbitrarily selected act which holds no direct bearing on one's worldly pursuits save what time's lost conducting it, is as a singular anchor at sea. It's to harvest a fistful of purposelessness at a regular interval to the end of reconfiguring purposelessness' presence as an obstacle. To unwaveringly adopt any small ritual is to guarantee an inviolable iota of purchase at what point in a twenty-four hour period it's practiced — the whole of oneself temporarily in step with the main vein devoid of sense underpinning all that is, and a kind of alignment on the order of being well-rested following one's nightly imitation of death, thereby achieved.

Though not directly comparable given the physiological imperative of sleep, consciously implemented ritual could be said to leverage the stabilizing force of that and other involuntary cycles, at the higher biological echelon where decision-making takes place. It doesn't particularly clarify anything on an intellectual level — but it alleviates the perceived obligation to internally articulate one's perceptions in non-contradictory terms. As far as carrying on with interpersonal interaction, a baseline of linear reasoning is advisable — but becoming comfortable with abandoning it when it's tying knots too tightly to employ a thereto unseen variety of creative problem solving for the sake of sanely and consistently staying one's individual course, begins with the controlled, private, voluntary embrace of the meaningless. It's a whetstone for honing negative capability.

Often that finds form in people's lives in ways they might only be capable to interpret as shameful or time-wasting, in which case one might possess a compulsive relationship with it — the notion of its being safe and useful hidden behind the scab they've created flagellating themselves each time it's accessed as a release valve in fits of tension. In every situation, the fine aperture one detects containing insight to the optimal angle of approach will often present as little more than a lacking solution on its own. The mistake in dismissing those treacherously attained outcroppings offering themselves as alternatives to detour, is that one misses out on the discovery of undetected corridors providing simple and straightforward ground for the taking. The matter can be likened to investigating a parking space one vaguely suspects is taken, to find their suspicions affirmed, but the space behind it vacant; instead of cutting wide across the concrete field in either direction, effort is saved by virtue of one's determination to evaluate their options in strictly incremental descent using the first choice as ground zero.

It's common habit when striving to embody some newfound rhythm to revert back to the tendencies one's grown sick of — even though the untouched ground between the present position and the objective will never grant passage before one finds humility enough to honor the chronology of growth and abandon their established territory. As twisted as it seems, the wisest decision when a thing demanding half one's concern is ripped away is to use the pain as fuel to nurture the other half with undivided attention — one cannot trust themselves to undertake this if their standard approach to development is any less opportunistic than that of a vulture. The rationale is that to neglect the release of what could raze fields (the freed up energy previously committed to the cultivation of whatever's been destroyed) is to permit it to destroy one internally — and furthermore that though unsavory, it's one's prerogative to determine where it's siphoned. The willingness to use loss as a means of elevating focus is prerequisite to the mastery of its control.

To focus is to take responsibility for the consequences of spending one's energy; if one finds it impossible to leverage the gift of mental real estate upon which worry needn't further be cast — it's preposterous to suppose they'd effectively hone the attention at their disposal to its potential. The cultivation of discipline depends on one's ability to maximize their time regardless of what emotions arrive in tandem with its sudden enlargement. It follows that a commitment to anything is not merely a pact — but one necessarily to the exclusion of everything that would threaten to stand in the way of attending it. One knows no bond with anything before the resolve to spill blood stands before its violation. The utmost discrimination should be exercised in selecting how to spend each moment, not simply because there may come a time when it's necessary to bleed to maintain heading, but because age burns everyone's wick whether or not the endeavor at hand is deemed worthy, and one is only alive to the degree they'd willingly sacrifice.

There may be nothing healthier than the fear of an unworthy death. If what knots bind the pit of one's stomach do not coincide with the threatened wreckage of one's deliberately followed course, bow to it as a sign of some amount of dead weight about to be lifted. One fits their keyhole bare; if the cold isn't biting as viciously as the heat scalds and the thorns stick as one contorts themselves to appease the tumblers — it's sure what protective detritus one's draped over themselves for comfort stands in the way of proper alignment.

Decisive action is absolutely critical in the matter of bringing desired outcomes within reach — one should absorb themselves with the minutiae of their occupations past the point where what would normally strike one as remarkable doesn't so much as incite a shift in gaze. The plethora of details one is competent to cognize can be stripped from everything not posing bodily threat and crammed with room to spare into one's elected subdivision of proficiency. It's appalling to watch a creature with such huge reserves of perceptive and organizational capacities falter in delegating those resources in fervent accordance with their greatest intent, and alarming to witness the delicate sensitivity facilitating resplendence in its corresponding works, abused and overworked catering to the management of joys and sorrows entirely extraneous to the critically navigated depths involved with unearthing bona fide prowess.

The same way it's detestable to see the blood pressure of some elite animal fit to sprint the plains skyrocket on account of captivity, is it to exist among humans fiending after lanterns housing genies of cheap pleasure and rapid decay. Living without the intensity of a thing blessed to be at all is no trivial cause to flirt with suicide — the only act of equal opposite potency to giving form that raging force engendered in all life, is to invert the expression by snuffing life out. It's easy to coast in ignorance to the gravity of the matter — but that's merely the equivalent of orchestrating a slow asphyxiation, and over time no less reprehensible than blatantly deleting oneself with a projectile.

It's not without reason saying someone wouldn't hurt a fly is meant to imply the absence of destructive predilection at greater scales, or why one's disposition toward waitstaff is indicative of a more pervasive intolerance — the extrapolation of character traits is quite elementary to navigating people. Subsequently it's notable that the distance from center one strays in responding to discussions of death, mirrors the degree to which their persona is a vacant husk. The process of bringing one's actual self and one's desired self into uniformity cannot be without strain, for it depends on a voluntary, working relationship with the prospect of death. Especially if one seeks to make it happen at a still-vital age, what would otherwise be shed in the course of time is wisely discarded prior to being so ripe it's taken by external forces, and though the agony of whittling oneself is thorough — one stands in remarkable stead pending the cauterization of those wounds than would be the case if it were an accident opened them up.

Somewhat counterintuitively, falling flat following the way one personally opts to take is significantly easier to recover from than undergoing the same variety of mishap at the behest of another — but only because the pain of what lessons are learned have then no others to distribute itself among. One smokes themselves out of their own chrysalis in spreading the shock of some hard revelation over an area — to swallow its effects with no attempt to evade the excruciating sear, is to openly accept a bountiful harvest in disguise. When biting the bullet becomes play, everything one regards becomes saturated with sweetness, and gliding even over the molten rocks of hell without despair is feasible.

To become a conduit through which many pleasant things pass, one must regularly exercise the act of relinquishing. Letting-go is seldom seen as more than a method for circumventing the distasteful, but this perspective flies blind to the other side of the coin — that there's an abundance of joy that would course ceaselessly through one's system provided the appropriate clearance for its passage. To suppose hoarding flowers the best way to remain in their presence — one constructs a temple of rot. To take what comes as it comes, one must know the unrelenting anxiety of holding what's foreboding at the door, and the torturous sorrow of clinging to that which is past its time. This in mind, it's wise to only make promises fulfillable in the foreseeable future. Reckless declarations made in spite of time are as fearful threats from children made to rabid dogs. Standing against the backdrop of all that's ever transpired, one is hopeless to shape any pattern of note without acknowledging it as mere sandcastles in the tireless tide of the aeon. Only following the forthright salute of that ever-eroding force, may the work of a lifetime begin.

11

STILLNESS, RELATIONS

The relationship between stillness and movement emerges at a minimum with a set of points in a vacuum. There are always at least two points. Even if one imagines a void wherein a single object flits about — the subtle reality of its apparently solitary movement is that the observer, i.e., the imagining individual, constitutes the second point. It could also be conceived that any instinctively imposed borders that that point moves relative to, function as points in and of themselves. A vacuum possessed of a single point is indistinguishable from a vacuum possessed of no points as far as movement is concerned. So — two points in a vacuum initialize the conditions for movement, but because each is the measure for the other, it cannot be said which moves and which does not, or if both move. Three points in a vacuum is the minimum state for ascertaining the independent presence of both movement and stillness simultaneously. This in mind — movement as a phenomenon can only emerge at all when objects in space are conceptually distinct from one another.

By conceptually assimilating everything into a singular point, then, it becomes possible to dissolve into a state of impenetrable stillness. The value in exploiting this culturally unentertained abstraction is as a button for pausing distress. Untold utility rests in controlling the shift of the partition dividing what axes qualify as one's own from what do not, because it reduces the challenge of striking balance on an otherwise vertigo-fraught platform adrift in the thrashing waves of cosmic uncertainty, to a matter of taste.

The power to feel at home anywhere is ordnance at the disposal of each, with the catch of being akin in nature to Mjolnir; its manipulation cannot be taught — subservient exclusively to the will of its master. No other can force that emptiness behind the eyes into tune with its own malleability; it's a shifting vessel corralling its contents with such perfect instantaneous response that the only viable precondition for deliberately steering its effect is for its owner to participate in the good faith analysis of an unadulterated scoop of qualia — mapping the mind's passages which dictate the characteristic flow, what once imbibed, abides. To gauge the limits of a tool, it must be used with that intent.

Time cannot be without movement — it is a measure constructed on the basis of the various physical cycles. The entire drama of growth and decay can be held at bay insofar as one manages to engross themselves in the spirit of stillness, anxiety starved out by severing the preconscious connection to time's march. It is not, however, infallible reprieve to dwell past the threshold where what might be considered superficial material concern holds no sway. To be caught outside the binding of worldly affairs is to struggle vainly as a cat with its pride going by doors through which the potential acquisition of tuna fish perpetually beckons — divorce with desire postponed on account of danger's grip over the territory opposite the porch lights.

Spending time in that interstice beyond time is not without consequence if one fails to exit on the side facing death. For this reason, it's crucial to determine what specific personal eddies one seeks to dispel in dwelling where no knot holds fast — beneficial reconstitution only possible by leveraging that vanishing margin between those deep, equalizing waters, and the dazzling light show above them; retaining just enough involvement to hover above the void, and expelling just enough to remain unscathed under the open air — the optimal composition of interest concocted in preparation to gracefully resurface. It is a scrubbing of the slate, that what it reflects may be redrawn, only one loses their frantic urgency by stepping freshly into new flesh — the favoritism composing one facet of whatever conundrum prompted their evasion from their standard lot of chaos, abandoned just as necessarily as their hopelessness stemming from the conviction they might never release themselves from it.

There are myriad ways to access a state where past those moments preceding and following sleep may pass without angst — for in dead, solitudinous silence, the omens of latent strife are as impervious as regrets on a death bed, and prove in their presence or absence a decisive test of spiritual quietude. Perhaps the most common, if not best recognized method, is to take up an amount of forthright action to the end of bringing some vision into realization, prying enough space in the jamb between self and compulsion to permit freedom of navigation throughout one's options — their untainted assessment made feasible by virtue of the balance attained through muscling oneself to the point of longing for respite, but in service to something rationally desirable. At that central space it's easiest to drop into stillness — the unceasing pull toward degeneration and the cultivated momentum toward achievement canceling each other out.

Without starting with oneself as the nexus from which that stillness germinates, it's possible to feel oneself being torn around the lot of the world in uncontrollable orbit — the only thing at all not possessed of some justified relation. Just as foolish is it to read that scenario as one where everything else is out of hand, as though the self and the universe's center are synonymous on all fronts. Playing at the possibility of anything without lending credence to the entire swath of personal concerns relevant to it, in the ways they're indispensably factored and trivially consequential alike — is to blindly force oneself to land flat-assed on either of those sides, groping out of touch with the full body of the experience in a daze of self-importance or self-effacement. Channeling stillness or chaos or love or studiousness is all a matter of positioning oneself such

that those things might permeate the personal system —
holding them at arms length or under a microscope hoping
to take away anything greater than hollow musings is like
doing everything with a piece of food except eating it;
primates learn via mimicry.

To assess one's baseline of flexibility in this respect, see
how enthralled one can become dancing in silence out of
eyeshot. The gravity of the trance corresponds precisely
with how flush one may translate the intimation of a thing
into an actual experience. Note, though, it's quite possible
to be too open in this respect — the ultimate composure of
anything a matter of infinitely fine tuning, and dissolution
in cascades of excess empathy a threat no lesser than drying
up an isolationist. Considering as much as possible within
some domain before acting is to the full swath of human
endeavors as accumulating the requisite revolutions per
minute in a motor vehicle prior to shifting gears; it causes
loads of unnecessary strain to neglect, and just as much to
overcompensate with.

The dearth of replicable formulae for nailing the sweet
spot should not be used as an excuse to quit gunning
for it, but allowed to corral one out of identification
with the various conceptions through which the direct

experience of reality is filtered — particularly when what decorates the edges of the promising proper course appears novel. That which one feels should be focal is tainted in its ability to fill the vestibule of mind proportional to the prodding, violatory conditions derived from past experience one reflexively imposes upon it. An individual's internal blueprint is alive, and must be drawn to fit one's personal vision as finely prescriptive as a temple for its monks, or a barracks for its warriors. Areas in its composition that would detract from the unbroken fluidity of one's optimal germination need be demolished or repurposed just as thoroughly as where houses the main setting for energy expenditure need be nurtured in its every detail.

Without a foundation of internal scrutiny, a scaffolding of individual composition honed to a standard affecting one's net positive growth — no permanent or substantial augmentation can be expected in the rearrangement of external circumstances. Though they're in the range of influence — being concerned with them before calibrating oneself to taste is like sweating cosmetics or a shoe brand before having an engine that'll turn over or a single mile under one's belt. In any case — that the outward appearance of a thing is scuffed firstly in the event of most mishaps is evidence the efficacy with which one exercises control drops dramatically as it draws distal from an internal locus.

Discovering oneself caught up attending what's trivially consequential prior to configuring the guts of one's situation is principally for fear of sacrificing aesthetic appeal — not something popularly interpreted as valuable below what superficial layers constitute the epidermis of a thing. To have a seamless, candied crust upon whose insides are rotting (the degree to which it's enticing surely otherwise matched or outmatched by the stench) — like the perjury of the innocent needlessly misleads and discredits; the human core is a composite of sturdy but altogether mutable stuff. It's so for living creatures their outermost tendrils respond in kind to the quality of the innards, whether the former are directly attended or not. All things considered, using oneself as a tool to set an example instead of aspiring to the manipulation of peripheral phenomena is not only the most reliable way to ensure an adequate symbiosis between the many layers working in tandem which amount to a complete individual — but prevents the perpetuation of an image that it's wise to spend resources organically supplied to each for their own maintenance and refinement, on trivialities.

Learning by trial and error is like eating out of the trash, in that it's always advisable to find alternatives, but is unwise to forgo as the sole option at hand. That said, in the attempt of any feat which would, by one's own estimation, christen their existence as something remarkable — there is the stark and potent reminder that that which is regarded as trash differs from its counterparts only because the latter are rebranded. Indeed, the difference between anything served as fine dining, and an amount of roadkill which would sustain one just as effectively — is a matter of presentation.

To write one's own script does not mean to discredit what's been established, but to honor it by trying one's hand at mustering a significant contribution — almost inevitably by using whatever methods one finds themselves implementing faced with the methodologically insurmountable, i.e., by trial and error. It isn't as though what ore engulfs the pulsating nectar of novel beauty isn't always just around the corner, but some combination of the acknowledgment that its density is not overcome without a consistent maximization of willful effort, and the pressure involved with knowing oneself as who's responsible for taking charge of its excavation — which prompts its forfeit. Learning to walk a creative path, is, above all, to obliterate what mystical hopes and fears call one forth to do so. The body secures stasis with each kick of the legs after being submerged underwater; the shock of walking the walk dissipates with each correctly placed step. The dopaminergic jolt associated with some fabled action being close at hand can make an addiction out of the space just prior to attainment, because once the latter is discovered not only to bring that mouthwatering anticipatory tension under collapse, but a deluge of change alongside it, the illusion that self-sabotage is more economical as a reward system than genuine progress becomes subconsciously tantalizing — improvisation set aside as the fallback strategy pending disaster.

Where from the path one regularly strays is home, and so the solution to enjoying its nourishment without subjecting oneself to inhibitive obstruction of movement, is to fence it off in the bounds of one's boots. If it's luxury to live in an ever-voluminous palace, to walk the Earth without feeling apart from one's home is not only the mark of the ultimate nomad, but that of the wealthiest homeowner. It's a necessity configuring oneself as such that any gulch in which what afflicts one courses is categorized not as a feature of the outside world, but gouged from an unwittingly alienated section of oneself.

Really, since the self has the unique property that it's accurately described as both infinitesimal and infinite, nothing is plausibly so comparable to it that its differentiation from oneself ever unconditionally ceases to be feasible — but by that same token nothing is so distinct from oneself that it isn't assimilable as a portion of the identity. It is only possible to describe the self in any exclusive sense using negative statements, i.e., evaluations in terms of what it isn't — whether phrased

"it is not..." or

"it is not just..." That ineffable, undiscardable pit shirks all of what's tacked to it in the course of experience with the same ease as the light from one's eyes in the instant of death.

Whether perception is best described as a node versus a network thereof is a line of questioning which inevitably leads to the exaltation of both possibilities; the latter forces one into wonder regarding the truth of cohesion, and whether the implication that it's possessed as an inextricable feature of the atrocity and exploitation which plague it doesn't lend credence to the merit of an isolated reasoning apparatus poised to rebel against the currents of the great sick organism; the former beckons inquiry into the ontological variability of that intangible void within which the node is an island — and if the fact that that island's ever-present opposing shores are all of what floods its senses can be conscionably disregarded in the assertion of what it *basically is*. The constriction of anything living appears to be just as principal to its quality as the character of its expansion — the road on which to walk, the muck through which to slog, the air (resistance) through which to soar, as it were. Without some challenge from under which one learns to struggle with a sense of dignity, life is as alarmingly bland and featureless as a toddler's playpen to an adolescent.

At intervals one may, depending on their emotional constitution, impose upon themselves an excess of strife in spite-filled retaliatory tantrums against what woes the world has thereto presented them with. Such behavior befits, and arguably even indicates a certain strength to be admired — in a child. Once the artificial veil of safety lifts at pace with the innocence lost in coming of age, however, that same behavior turns from innocuous and charming to uncouth and impractical. Though borne of the same emotional seed — the upset endemic to a kid disposing of their own toys or deliberately writing extra lines out of enmity when punished, matures into little more than bedlam on the course to the senseless emptying of magazines into air over a battlefield, or the trashing of hard-won acquisitions in incorrigible frustration.

Notably, used as a means of protest, its effectiveness makes it ubiquitous. The difference between a child or a protester and an adult going about the course of their existence, are the implied coordinates of responsibility. The former examples use their expectation of acknowledgment to secure a beneficial position relative to what entities they believe responsible for their well-being, whereas such flirtation with destruction for the latter, would, by being in perfect contravention to the course of what human progress they muster, and for whom no others are functionally accountable — effectively constitute insanity. To boot, since in today's age any sliver of competence is often sufficient to afford one some station of responsibility for others, or at the very least one integral to the structural integrity of a team — one is complicit in the suffering of those whose efforts uphold them insofar as they childishly cast off their own provisions in lieu of figuring out ways to reinvest them.

Life is requisitely one of service because it is *spiritually suicidal* to expect solutions to be cast down from someplace on-high. Fraught with embellishment and New Age undertones as it is — to clarify, the notion of "spirituality" is used here the same way as "physicality." Just as the latter is a high-level sum of many individual mechanisms, divisible into things like lats, quads, VO2 max, agility, and so forth — the former is the same, but for the intangible and/or subjective human qualities which are often brazenly redacted from the roster of traits perceived subservient to personal control, such as temperament, attentiveness, drive, dispositional stability, and joyfulness. It's the case while endeavoring to submerse oneself into any given spiritual solution that the ad-hoc composition of apparently immaculate arguments against choking-down what new implements are at hand, appear indefatigably opportune. Two core points arise in consequence to this observation.

One is that since the arena hosting those irreconcilable conflicts between perspectives on spirituality almost solely contain bouts of intellectual debate, it must be that the stage itself is unmitigably upheld by the stakes of either contestant's spiritual interests, rather than serving themselves, as might be expected, as their champions' weapons; there is apparently no quantity of strict reasoning that would allow one to undermine the foundations of their own spirit, provided it's serving them. The other necessarily follows the last, and is a clarification of the reason why every spiritual edifice demands some form of practice, methodology, or explicit manner of thinking or observing in order for its essence as a medicament to be imbibed — because the presently dissatisfactory faculties of mind expected to configure *themselves* into a superior state of organization is, without some such commitment, a laughable affront to what entropic forces forced it into the scattered mess posing the issue. In other words — though it can't be said one bears no responsibility for the contents of mind, those contents are unalterable without a modicum of faith in some foreign formula.

It's true if let alone for long enough that the body's capacity to heal itself can remediate considerable damage. That said — there are indubitably times where the sagest advice is to take advantage of external remedies. Primeval fledgling the corpus of comprehensive discourse concerning the myriad approaches to soothing the problems behind the eyes is, the language across cultures who've managed to arrive at identical solutions using different methods (ostensibly varying applications of the body's intrinsic healing capabilities as well as the implementation of medicaments) under different circumstances with different people in accordance with different intervals — presents on the whole as the wildly unpredictable and contradictory amalgam irreducible in anything newly born. Unweaving and re-weaving it into a conceptual lattice of general applicability is not the same easy task as getting everyone on the same page with the rapid complexification of techno-chemical warfare, because the global anxiety prompting the extermination of outward problems vastly outpaces that prompting the deliberate imperilment of whatever sacred improvisations toward internal peace each manages to hash together through the fog and confusion humanity's consecutive self-inflicted aftermaths kick up — for the sake of galvanizing a shared place of rest. Metaphorically, the matter fits quite nicely in the confines of a "simple" two-person relationship — what shell-shock and subsequent coping strategies each party's undergone and taken up on account of trials past, seems to constitute the mass not optionally waded through for both to honestly, openly, mutually acknowledge their bed as a legitimate place of respite.

The particular flavor of immaturity Earth's gifted problem children presently contend with appears to be that of an older adolescent. The revelation still tender that the bottom line means one must reason, fight, love, and be accountable on one's own behalf, they're therefore still distant from, and perhaps even antagonistic respecting, the prospect of shouldering the full gravity of that sacred rite of passage tied up in getting tied up with another and fulfilling the conditions for bringing what's new and wonderful to pass. The figure of sexual irresponsibility is safely extrapolated to represent the foundational crisis in creative endeavors on the whole, regardless of the domain in question — because sex is the most elementary example of a productive human system. Barring an attempt at objectively measuring the quality of either — at the very least, attitudes relating to the various stages of the basic creative union are liable to be reflected in the corresponding stages of other modes. How exactly such a thing would be realized en masse on a scale of eight-billion people is remarkably unclear.

Though the line of reasoning in the mid-twentieth century, that augmenting the cultural object of sexual union to include an ever-increasing number of participants might magically eradicate hardship, seems naive, conceptually reductionistic, and altogether impractical — perhaps since the prospect of widespread communicative clarity respecting the expectations of propagative human endeavor lies in the direction of catalyzing growth, it and every other conceivable configuration should at least be rekindled as open topics of unembarrassing, inoffensive discussion.

Tender and horrifying as it is for so many, there is little as personally relevant, yet as simultaneously ambiguous as a social structure, as sex. What's happened surrounding it in recent years is interesting, because instead of attempting to harbor discourse, the emotional boundaries surrounding any deviation from the one (1) biologically male, one (1) biologically female, monogamous, faithful, everlasting romantic arrangement — were (largely) surreptitiously bypassed for as long as the internet wasn't fostering anonymous expression, then unabashedly declared irrelevant by those who surfaced beyond them thereafter. The key point in this entire situation is language; by circumventing the common, almost always religious verbiage of the traditionalists, new frontiers came at the price of conceptually irreconcilable discord.

Using the parent-child dynamic to highlight the chronology of the phenomenon, discarding any suggestion of unidirectional authority — it's as if without warning one's son or daughter tore off indignantly to some foreign land under the cover of night without coherent explanation, then returned to argue their points in the unstudied tongue native from whence they came, fractionally appreciative of the linguistic rift they themselves went out of their way to pry for the sake of avoiding the vulnerability they'd be forced to contend with had they molted in the face of their loved ones. It is unequivocally the shared responsibility in any relationship of any type between all parties to celebrate, debate, reconcile, and conduct all other manner of interaction, with the utmost diligence to make use of preexisting shared conceptions as the scaffolding upon which anything new is introduced — otherwise it is the solitary burden of the voluntarily extricated member(s) to fare without the continued support of that collective. To put into perspective *why* those who elect novel ideas into the established network are obliged to uncomplainingly face the music of *their* alienation — it is because growth which transpires before a direct, earnest, successful appeal to the elders at whose behest one benefits from the communal levies, is *fundamentally cancerous*. That is to say, it is *mechanistically identical* to the development of cancer in a living organism. It is possible attain a status warranting collective renown and praise using the exact same principles and implements ripe wherever one seeks to annex new territory, if only one honors the minimum girth of the stem keeping them connected. Too often do people cast themselves untethered into the pits of chaos in search of freedom from the framework which binds them, only to find that escape from those pits anyway requires the forfeit of total freedom, and indeed that life integrated as part of something greater is a thing of ceaseless reciprocity.

On the contrary, it is similarly the duty of those aforementioned elders to proactively mine from the calciferous protection of their set ways, a minimum of respect, honor, and appreciation for the inspirations possessed by the frontier generations, for though the latter are charged with invigorating the system wherefrom they sprout, so too are they enlivened by the glistening allure of the possibilities they perceive — possibilities cut, in all actuality, from the same cloth composite to what fueled the laborious tilling of the soil supporting what infrastructure cradles its original masters through their old age.

12

DRAWING THE LINE

I nnovation is proactive maintenance. The reason it's difficult to transform is because there's confusion surrounding what fundamentally constitutes an upgrade; it's nothing more than the implementation of a longer than average term fix to a given problem. The confusion, basically, arises in consequence to the paradoxical juxtaposition of the gratification experienced during the attainment of progress, and its futility in light of increasing timescales. Whether one bleeds cries or sweats any blood sweat or tears trying to reconcile that paradox — not a singular human decision is made without exertion through the tension it presents.

The average size of the buffer one commands conducting maintenance in a given domain, beginning with a minimum avoidance of imminent catastrophic failure, and pushing into the limitlessly nascent chaos of the future, indicates (relative to the set of all buffers in that domain) their attitude concerning gratification and futility.

Since it comprises both the chief blunder in situations where hopelessness is focal, and the chief virtue given the opposite — how one feels on the whole about the act of maintenance itself, without context, functions as the ideal litmus test for revealing their most thoroughly pervasive notion of life in its entirety. As the neutral zone between play and drudgery, wherefrom it's approached conceptually tells the tale of one's native perceptions. It's something of a paradigmatic prism, refracting in accordance with its angular relationship to any given observer, the implications bound therein permeable though not manipulable by rationale — all assessments of it, then, the product of a deeper, more primary interface, such that no degree of intellectualization is required to instantiate any as of yet unpracticed expression of it. In other words, there is the ever-present possibility that play could instantaneously undergo an experiential conversion into war on any arbitrarily selected front, and vice versa, via the casual rotation of what presuppositions maintenance is attended with.

It being so that no bounds exist to restrict what's gone south from getting worse, or what's gone well from continuing to improve — all that differentiates extremes of either is how the opposite is interpreted as a supporting role. Locked into some fulfilling engagement, that which would otherwise impede one's spirit functions to catalyze further interest by providing a suitable amount of friction to give the endeavor at hand form, whereas when struggle is central, what quantity of hope and positive progress is undergone serves only to highlight the inescapable gravity of its counterpart — at peak insidiousness justifying the nihilistic satisfaction milked from destruction as the only tenable motivator. Far as colored glasses from what's considered foundationally constituent to reality as such concepts are — the very limits of exploration are dictated by what means one possesses to swap lenses, so to speak, lest the habituated imposition of a given perspective render one impotent to evade the obstacle of a mental quandary, defenseless against the affliction of learned helplessness.

Striving to stab one's own preferences to a cork board, twisted gratification it promises — is hardly more than the employment of shackles to scratch an itch. Sure — in the final analysis, the alternative of freedom may not qualify as ultimately preferable to whatever effrontery to genuine growth one elects to substitute for its transformatively scathing flames, but to pare-down one's body of concern until it inhabits no more than the space afforded by a contest between any quantity of desirable options, then referring thereafter to the process of their selection as an exercise in "freedom," is a grievous misappropriation of the term. The actual apprehension of freedom means constant conflict with substantial threats, because in a cascading lasagna of systems, the capacity for unbridled expression means war with whatever barriers compose the upper limit below which one finds themselves capable to transcend.

To occupy oneself with trivial problems is likewise to trivialize one's potential for expansion; the pain of becoming anything new and the pain of watching oneself wither, merely playing at invested involvement — are interchangeable. Notice how in any case, reasoning tight to either end of a polarity breeds attitudes in line with the aforementioned trivialization. For example, concerning the matter of fate versus free-will — a preferential tilt toward the former progressively justifies any behavior, and similarly one leaning acutely toward the latter, in relinquishing themselves from any semblance of a biological, historical, social, religious, scientific, etc., structure, accomplishes the same. It's feasible to ascertain the application of any such axis (fate/free-will, good/evil, individuality/group values) to the end of inciting a binary collapse of reasoning an act of such hyper-simplification that it's actually what caps the otherwise endlessly increasing resolution at which any given situation can be analyzed. It is the evolved solution of a chimp throwing its scat.

It is also completely unavoidable, except for in what one resolves to do until their dying breath — if one manages to confine some division of their energy into a process demanding perpetual countermanding and reform. One's death at their chosen workbench before an unfinished project, then, is the highest expression of humanity — as it represents an ultimately victorious battle against the unending instinctual entreaty to throw one's arms in the air in declaration of the lot of life as rightly relegated to the lavic bowels of Satan's boiler-room. That seems, in fact — to be the very nectar of what's called *honor*. Its meaning, in the current age marred and caked with implacable notions of mindless suffering at the behest of mass-manipulators, before the means to feverishly clamber over one another without consequence to assert the inherent supremacy of any given ideology were so universal — itself represented the common merit of every person who simply did what they did without paying mind to external forces, and without a lick of reservation.

It's tricky to see what value lies there when so often arguments transpire at the scale of what *ought* to be done, and yet the picture of anyone possessed of unwavering persistence *doing* virtually anything out in the open is positively riveting. So though celebrated to some degree, what's been lost along with that notion's divorce from its denotive term, "honor," is something like efficacy of the justificatory crankshaft serving to transfer the awe inspired by an individual into the wheels of society and culture at large as a mutually integrated cause for excitement and aspiration, toward which any could strive to emulate free from backlash — assured simultaneously of personal recognition, and the potential to hold a station of collective importance as a contributor of great works.

Part of what's difficult in delineating honor's worth
is assigning a quantifiable metric uniformly across the
spectrum of accomplishment in a way which reliably
isolates that virtue from whatever other possibly incendiary
points of consideration someone's efforts may bring to
bear. Arguably, it's blatantly irresponsible to lend intrinsic
credence to what's essentially stubbornness unlashed to a
more explicit evaluation of the parameters within which it's
acceptable, but as something fruitfully practiced and easily
accessible to anyone keen on adopting it without definite
schemes respecting its weaponization, it's completely
reasonable to regard the ceaselessly churning maelstrom
of suppositions wherein it's intractably some flavor of
transgression, as basically adversarial — not to suggest that
warrants completely ignoring it. It's intuitive to gun for an
acceptable minimum of chaos consequential to one's focus,
but what one finds continuing diligently enough down
any given rabbit-hole of relevant tangential possibility, is
that to draw the line anywhere is to draw blood; linear
progress is realized in inverse proportion to one's total
breadth of attention, hence why on average those capable
of deliberately bringing change to bear in brief windows
can tend to come off as abrasive — one for whom a

week is thrice as dense as another's in development along some metric may deliberately relegate entire domains of experience intimately significant for that other into the category of near-complete ignorance.

Attention is stressed as the primary faculty here because it constitutes the aperture through which energy loss manifests as activity — across time observably responsible as the function controlling one's course through existence, much the same way one's teeth over the course of a meal serve to separate what's consumed (what becomes of one) from what's rejected. Instead of taking its ingestive role as something externally dictated, which is the equivalent of succumbing to a grand caloric surplus with the attitude that since there's a feast at hand, one is choiceless in the matter — one establishes ever-more control over their particular orientation every time they act against the impulse to commit themselves to rationally subordinate qualia. More often than not, regardless of how the undesirable urge manifests — what occurs is the usurpation of physiologically registered concern from what's intended, resulting in the type of jarring dissonance one would undergo with "WRONG WAY" signs flitting past on the genuinely proper route to their scheduled destination.

Successfully discerning the optimal means of recourse when one comes upon ravines gashed between time spent occupied with what's of calculated import, aside from instantly circumventing them (reflexes permitting) — is wholly predicated on the proficiency with which one can pull themselves into a state of disengaged relaxation. Fair bet scrambling mad to retake the cusp off which one's only just stumbled, but once there's the ungraspable inch between it and the furthest outstretched fingertip, the criteria for conjuring a solution totally inverts. In anything — when evasion becomes synonymous with postponement, it's necessary to dilate one's attention so as to construct a response derived from a more disparate repertoire of potential maneuvers.

Another way of conceptualizing the matter is to imagine a sandy, rocky slope, up which one struggles to climb. If the linear path from the bottom-most point to the plateau, somewhere along which one claws incessantly upward, is tractionally insufficient to facilitate gainful ascension — the singular best course of action is to quit wasting energy struggling and sit in still observation of the situation. The anxiety coloring whichever perch one manages to hold onto from that juncture is twofold; on one hand there's the stress of falling from wherever one is, and on the other there's the stress of making progress and subsequently falling from an even greater height. In light of this, one sees that not only would further movement directly upward be counterproductive on account of the slope's inherently treacherous navigability — but doubly-so given the e-brake unconsciously activated on behalf of one's preservative instincts in resistance to the danger of exacerbated fall damage.

From *there*, the situation's difficulty is effectively halved, considering half the strain handled had been the product of wholly governable sabotage. The repercussions of this miscalculation are mitigable insofar as one manages to rest into their footholds, as in any case the human propensity for suffering extends to ground untaken in the form of regret, in addition to measurable wounds; the latter being a coin-flip, while the former is guaranteed to assail one in full force before one hits the ground — it finally makes *more* sense to continue upward in some lateral fashion from wherever one sits, in lieu of losing ground acting out the subconscious dictates of fear.

Moving past what's been causing delay is always a choice between a route adjustment and remaining patient. In the case of creative pursuits particularly, or likewise efforts whose fruition depends on a certain capacity to tunnel through unknown territory, plotting the course as one proceeds — staying put invariably produces the same effect as giving up. The guise of patience is a lethally suffocating mask under such conditions, because it's the point-man's sole responsibility to establish an immediate way forward. Another means to conceptualize the matter is as a spelunker; standing by for an indication to continue after failing to discover any adjacent chambers is conducive to respite (albeit indirectly), but the task at hand remains — incessant exploration is mandatory in the attainment of novel progress.

Life is something like a consecutive series of frontiers at which each is obliged to gamble. Even safe bets are only safe insofar as they're stabilizing — traded for them oftentimes is a sense of fulfillment. On the contrary, to roll the dice on a dream never leaves one with a dearth of tales to tell, but the likelihood of whatever vein of normalcy binding one to the physical plane respecting relationships, sustenance, a relatively unvaried daily average of strife undergone, and the litany of other benefits taken as unforgoable matters of course to any and all content to exist sans the masochism involved with birthing new combinations of matter, becoming as positively unwoven as a fish in a blender — can hardly be overstated.

The cultivation of indifference before varying circumstances is ultimately what renders it feasible to fine-tune the personal apparatus; the details of one's bloom can be uninterruptedly discriminated in their minutiae so long as the sanctum within which it's cultivated is impenetrable to the turbulence of external phenomena. Above all else, sustained commitment to a given set of actions is what defines a person. Whether or not what's committed to is correct is secondary to whether it's what's consciously elected — benevolence is hollow in one who's never had to choose it to the exclusion of anything dark and tempting, just as a bear's brutality is as good as innocence having lived its life without incentive to conduct itself differently.

Humans have the right to trust their own judgment because one sees the board in its totality as efficaciously as any other — mutual accountability enforced by that same token. As such, blame can only be shirked to the degree humanity is forfeited; to approach human apotheosis is to maintain a steady course in the midst of chaos, for chaos contains the undifferentiated amalgam of every conceivable eventuality, and if entirely shouldered permits one to conscionably isolate a path to the deliberate exclusion of all others. Those who've done this are charged with the task of leading other humans — the communal repertoire of viable patterns thereby augmented. Competitiveness is intrinsic to the human experience because it's impossible to shut oneself out from the teacher called chaos, and so life as a classroom is quite accurately a gradating roster of those who commit their attention that they may delineate their preferred approach, and those who cling to the faultlessness they're born with, striving to remain ignorant before the ever-compounding necessity to take on personal responsibility. The latter, generally speaking, tend to bear the marks of addiction, intellectual apathy, emotional instability — inertial comorbidities with one's lack of success in attaining ground amid the storm. Any of the aforementioned afflictions are generally remedied in tandem with the whole picture of a person, because their manifestation is indicative of chaos' presence in the depths of the spirit — overcoming them synonymous with the ability to hold fast in its face.

Perhaps the foremost barrier to successfully careening one's way through the fog is the erroneous presupposition, or even just the intimation, that anything *must* be done. It places weight on the external world in a way which binds actions to the expectation of perfect existential solution rather than their utility to satisfy the facets of human longing in their entire range from intensely pressing to simply convenient. Living without obligation can present a fearfully imposing obstacle at first, because dependence on functionally omnipotent reprimand as an orienting instrument is a common practice in youth. Beyond the organized societal structures through which that propellant is effective to move one, however, the spite-filled plaque accumulated resulting from that kind of worry-driven motivation, on account of the drag it produces, quickly saps the fine precision indispensable for remaining inside the bounds of the road one chooses to follow — which inevitably weaves in accord with the more diverse considerations accessible to a fledged creature.

The sensation of urgent necessity, unless bound to serve a timeless scheme, can be insidious in its potential to prevent the accumulation of forward momentum. Sat atop one's psychological throne, engaged in a ceaseless tirade of belittlement as though one's still-diaphanous wishes would ever be functionally striven for in a spirit of enslavement, it inhibits the peace of mind useful for making rational decisions by force-feeding an inadequate selection of near-term means by which to reach a given objective — the objective itself constructed out of anxious haste. The result of entertaining a variable goal using a toolkit rushed in its composition is an exhaustive, fruitless voyage through the hellish, ever-spawning weeds of intellectual overhaul — details at every angle demanding attention because they're incorrigibly at odds with one's true, comprehensive intent, and subsequently misaligned with the curiosity meant to organically lubricate consistent focus. The overload of stress due to the apparent absence of measurable headway juxtaposed with the increasingly frantic criticality of each new timeline eventually causes one to bail into the safety of comfort and/or hedonism. Then, as guilt creeps back onto the scene, the process repeats itself.

It is of course the case that to cash it in for a more stable base from which to proceed is to exchange those intermittent splurges for the paced trek of a lifetime — swapping the small wins and losses focal for one beholden to their compulsive urgency, with a singular all-in bet on the hand played from that instant to the grave, when otherwise the failure to exist according to some such conviction bites back with the force of a thousand regrets. The phantom in question masquerades as though it's concerned with precisely that avoidance of regret, but rather than serving to the end of its genuine amelioration, it entices one to surrender their faculties for the vague but immediate promise of arriving *somewhere* by acting with all speed. The gratification it offers is superficial in the same sense as a feeling of ownership derived from paying interest.

It isn't difficult to stake anything on an experientially fleeting moment among a sea of fleeting moments, because the impossibility of conceptually binding them together makes forthcoming disaster just as immaterial as progress. To stake the sum of one's energies on a premeditated trajectory in the present and lock in is terrifying, because instead of playing life by ear, one must deliberately poise for encounter with the insane increase of consequences and opportunities likely to present themselves across the full length of their newly fleshed-out model of the future — forcing an immediate and oftentimes dramatic renovation of behavior and habit. To commit oneself to a blueprint derived from the same mind content to toss itself headlong into scathing, perfectly avoidable misfortune, understandably creates contention surrounding the matter of whether to have faith in it — but the alternative is nigh-guaranteed self-destruction. Ignoring problems in hopes they'll disappear is like trying to remedy a revolver pointed between the eyes by shutting them tightly and praying to spontaneously manifest the object permanence of a five-month old.

Moving from a position of dubious footing to one of confidence-inspiring leverage when presented with novel problems requires the marriage between a charged nervous system and a clear mind. To have a tepid impetus for physical participation while the mind burns rubber — undercommitted countermeasures become the hammer with which whatever has presented itself will be handled; if the mind loses its lucidity while adrenaline and cortisol surge unchecked — the opposite transpires. The situation may work itself out in either case, but the point is that that likelihood is reduced to a coin-flip with half one's system taxed in compensation for the whole.

It is easy to confound a gut sensation which should be trusted, with compulsive urges, and therefore the ability to act on one's calculated differentiation between the two is the primary onus for each determined to cut clear through the excess raucous generated by abstraction and distraction alike. Without the luxury of having one's purpose thrown in their face, or if no sufficiently serene stasis wherein it could be teased from the depths of one's conscience has come to pass — know only that as one grows, the inevitability of expressing a single particular pattern becomes increasingly imminent, and though it'll be unavoidably characterized by what's undergone from birth, the present undertaking alone conceals the key to seizing fulfillment.

Enough energy is wasted clarifying one's position to others with more than the steady, inconspicuous application of personal principles and intentions; to writhe spitefully attempting to justify oneself before external expectations rather than abiding or abandoning them directly, betrays an unmistakable lack of diligence in cleansing the cognitive filters responsible for the efficient digestion of what's personally relevant, and conversely, for the reliable expulsion of what isn't. There's too much data not to run it through some such discriminatory system; at the very least, advice and criticism should be taken in kind with one's appreciation for from whom it comes.

13

CONFLICT, BLIGHTED RITES

C haracteristic of conflict is that each perceived transgression serves to instigate a counteraction liable to be perceived as transgressive unto itself — causing a pattern of compounding effect likenable to gravity. From one perspective, aggressiveness could be reasoned the degree to which one interprets instances of the aforementioned "counteraction" to be intentionally threatening, which preserves the innocence of the initially crossed — but interestingly from there, aggression could be simplified as the proclivity toward feeling threatened on the whole, counterintuitively implying that to undergo fear, despite its physiological deployment as what's considered a line of defense, *is* the initial condition for spinning up contention. In any case, the mark of the basically aggressive is the ease with which they'll enter into a state of indignant defense concerning their basis of retaliation. Via its reinforcement with implicit petitions for sympathy in place of standing calmly behind the intrinsic validity of one's actions, a subtle yet potent trap is set by making the opportunity to personally offend difficult to avoid — as any explanation rendered therefrom, accompanied by apology or not, disparages the emotional validity of the volatile party.

Since the basis of transgressive behavior is one-half dependent on the possibly offended party's conception of their own boundaries, there's just as much good faith required on their part to figure out and clearly communicate their own limits, as there is of everyone expected to remain vigilant on their behalf — as they've the ability to instantaneously shift their property line, so to speak, to territory miles beyond the point where anyone and their actions may be wholly encompassed. An aggressor's manifestation, in every case emerging as a response to disconcerting stimuli, and reasonably by extension interpretable as defensive, is difficult to definitively categorize as predatory. In observing that matter and energy can only be reconfigured as opposed to created or destroyed — it would be in error to think that life isn't inherently inevaluable as a zero-sum phenomenon; nature, as such, is autocannibalistic.

Divorced as such a high-level analysis may seem compared to a scene of gnashing teeth and entrails, where mountain lions and bunny rabbits unmistakably fulfill their respective roles as predators and prey — the fact that a lion never chooses to hunger draws its position equal to that of the hare. It's so throughout the human sphere that the most egregiously violent are those who voluntarily remain weak — or worse yet act to reinforce their identity as basically impotent. The weaker one is, the more they're likely to register as threatening to the point that violence appears a justifiable response. Leaving one's inability to progressively negotiate threats unmended is dangerous and irresponsible; straying from a genuine representation of what's deleterious, in any direction, unnecessarily contributes to the greater volatility of one's existence.

Granted it's damage for which any incite discord to begin with, from the perspective of the offending party, any implicit vulnerability central to reactions against their offense not only serves to confirm it's warranted (otherwise their subject would perceive no threat) — but adds insult to whatever injury stoked their actions, as their pain is not only denied but suggestively weaponized against them. It's not necessarily a factor at all whether the initial wrong could be viably pinned on whoever receives the burden of its correction. This difficulty, generally speaking, persists until anyone admits fault with enough effect to evoke a similar admission from the opposing party, someone dies, or each in earnest bids to hunt for the origin of their conflict either identify it as a misunderstanding or decide on some third entity to blame. Panic displayed in the attempt to avoid fault not only demonstrates a dysfunctional comprehension of human nature — but by extension a fundamental misunderstanding about what it is to be alive.

If the experience of guilt at another's expectation of repentance is taken to automatically indicate personal wrongdoing, one only allows themselves half the picture. At the bottom of it, that other is just as damned for their reckoning as who they condemn. Consider each, living so the majority of their time is spent enjoying a degree of stability sufficient to stave off rapid physical deterioration

— a common thread between virtually every living person. Quite arguably faultless as humans get their start, bundles of innocence infants are — notice that in the instant of their emergence, they are irreversibly sentenced to death. The point is that contention between those serving life sentences is always conducted on equal footing. There can be no expectation that any threat should go unreciprocated just because it's justified in the context of a provisional system; the finitude of life, on which any could fall back as a reason to do anything, means any imposition of order onto behavior is only viable insofar as it's explicitly agreed upon, otherwise one's foisted ideals are liable to be met with nothing less than the looming menace of death's expedited arrival, under which circumstances guilt is about as useful as a safety pin in a spear fight.

It's functional as an alert to shift approach where there's an interconnecting system of support reinforced consequential to specific undertakings — but inversely proportional to the length of time one goes on experiencing it, similar to how an audible alarm loses its salience should it blare continuously for hours straight. Racking oneself with guilt over long periods is like remaining stopped at a green light to apologize for running a red. The necessity for change is to be heeded, not used to attain recognition. It's a waste of everyone's time and makes a criminal of anyone who deigns to continually sympathize with those who decorate themselves with, as opposed to gainfully transmuting, their lapses of judgement — hence the social isolation of the pathologically guilt-ridden.

Unease, irritability, confusion — uncomfortable as they are, they're half the recipe for carrying out commendable action. Crude analogy it may be, shelving those feelings is sure to breed apathy the same way removing one's legs would — they're imperative for overcoming the obstacles they germinate in response to. Prolonged guilt and self-sabotage walk hand in hand because the former represents claws retracted for fear of causing harm — without which no hunting can be done. It is an enormous mistake to forget the ultimate price is requisitioned upon parturition, because it's information which permits one to *move on*.

Reasoning as though the first-person experience doesn't totally eradicate the possibility of pure altruism is quite like extolling the virtues of silence through a megaphone. It's not only hypocritical, but in so discordantly flaunting what directly impedes the consciously calculated implementation of the alleged intent, one is prone to lose track of why communal service makes sense in the first place, and consequentially lash out in a stiff one-eighty against whichever force prompted them into their frantic elopement with half the point. Filing for divorce from a trajectory of personal gain renders it impossible to conduct oneself in earnest or with any great effect — especially philanthropically, since the demands of its participation are one-to-one with what's been personally attained. On the contrary, to possess a laundry list of narcissistic tendencies constipates the capacity to *receive* love, or more specifically to register the effect of anything less superficial than what vain acknowledgment such a one doles out in order to maintain an air of relative likability.

Mirroring the aforementioned maladjusted relationship with guilt, confusion concerning whether to give or to take can become an eddy unto itself, especially considering the highest form of empowerment is ostensibly to reveal those dormant skills with the potential to foster independent competence — often counterproductively overshadowed by generic gifts which enable unchecked comfort and idle pleasure. The quite uniform infatuation with education in the modern world is expressive of a collective intuition that there's space between grueling labor and monetary inheritance which exalts a person to the highest degree — though though its essence shines through in form, the pay-to-play system it's devolved into is an inhibitive blight to what starry-eyed ambitions young initiates approach it with. The dissonance of finding oneself newly engulfed in an institution to whom absurd quantities of resources are signed away at the behest of allegedly responsible, upright, knowing adults, only to find it fraught with precisely the kind of limbic degeneracy it's designed to buffer — is as reprehensibly inflicted as the abandonment of a puppy having joyously fetched their favorite toy from some novel backcountry, only to find the distant taillights of their entire world receding into forever down the unfamiliar strip of asphalt they were released upon with the promise of an engaging afternoon not twenty seconds prior.

The interstice between childhood and adulthood is hardly traversable without what's essentially a committal disguised as a rite of passage, the latter only truly completed once one develops the wherewithal to successfully claw themselves out of whatever culturally sanctioned subdomain of insanity procured them the minimum permissible history of socially recognizable cooperation; as though a lifetime of blind obedience would ever imbue a human being with the prowess appropriate for one up to whom the following generations would be wise to look. Instead of placing weight on the necessarily transformative quality irreducible in a legitimate rite of passage, it's placed on the willingness to commit oneself to a length of indentured servitude — the recruiter's office and the freshman orientation laying on ever-thicker the assurance of dignification as one draws closer to the event horizon.

It isn't so that such institutions are universally or entirely cesspools — but if there's tangibly glib emphasis on its various features of prestigious iconography *to the exclusion* of demonstrably rigorous and compelling environments of development, it rests on its laurels enough to warrant concern. Part of what makes combating such complacence difficult from the inside is the tendency of collectives to reinforce excuses useful for avoiding strain; the propagation of mediocrity is like a warm blanket which grows wider and more tranquilizing with each additional member enveloped in its folds. It's necessary to become borderline antisocial under such conditions if maintaining a standard is something one finds personally paramount — what cold winds one exposes their peers to in ripping oneself from that comfort almost guarantees the commencement of demands for one to voluntarily undergo some form of sedation.

Doing something is better than doing nothing, and doing nothing is better than being distracted. Starve what vies for attention and it will be forced to reveal itself in its true form if it's intent on continuing to hold its stake in the personality. Note that only a parasite needs to conceal itself at mealtimes, so paying attention to what replaces any choice diversion is worthwhile; fair shot the quantity of energy wasted on it will appear deserved of no less than a full-service funeral thereafter.

14

RECONCILIATION

It's difficult to reason about the dichotomy between free-will and determinism, because should the latter constitute the reality of the situation — the pre-orchestration of every point posited robs them of their gravity no matter which angle they reinforce. Luckily, to assert "the reality of the situation" any which way is secondary to the experiential precedence of being conscious, which precludes the seamless integration of mere concepts. What's primary is subtly revealed in the very notion that two fundamentally opposing perspectives might be pitted against eachother in this way: uncertainty. Granted, even to assert epistemic peril as the bedrock of experience does not erase the deadlock presented by the potential of a deterministic reality, but as the minimum increment for escaping total meaninglessness — it's the only viable option.

If one imagines a circle split in two with determinism and free-will occupying either side, it functions as the set of all sets, and is synonymous, as it were, with absolute chaos. Given a perpetual, unwinnable war, waged with means unconstricted by any form or theme whatsoever (the two sides not only exclude one another, but attempt to encompass the whole universe in their explanatory breadth) — the world and all its contents *are* the expression of that altercation. The largest concentric group within that last provides just enough purchase to facilitate the possibility of establishing order locally, and harbors the divide between the known and the unknown. If there is uncertainty, there must then be its complement.

Notice that the leverage gained by allowing personal volition a position of consequence in charging it with the discernment of clarity comes at the loss of an equivalent quantum of logical scrupulousness which is indispensable for fleshing-out the full brunt of the contradiction between free-will and determinism. Is it possible that this pattern extends in proportion to the depth at which one enters into the dramas constituting frontal experience — intuitively derived heuristics gradually replacing what models one employs to figure their environment, the perception of rational paradox something inversely related to that of involved understanding at a foundational level? Or is it rather the case that the notion of understanding should be further differentiated to accommodate both the disengaged indexing of causal relations, and the irreducible subjectivity of apparent phenomenological "alignment," alike?

Maybe the opposite approach, to blur the line between the felt versus the figured, makes the most sense; it's so that "ought" cannot be gleaned from "is," but is not the drive to categorize the world's features, if not an expression of what should be done, at the very least, as a consequence of the same human desire whose direction couldn't but run parallel with one's intimations of proper conduct — reveal the root between reason and feeling a shared thing, and thus the two hardly dissimilar? It seems whether to fret over the boundaries of some problem or to exhaust oneself actually engaged with it is a balance only attained in step with a particular rhythm over the course of time, because as concerns a singular situation — they're mutually exclusive. The process of creating anything shows how deploying the bottomless availability of some medium in tandem with the intermittent imposition of definite structural, visual, or sonic, etc., articulation, as exampled in cornices, outlines, breakdowns, etc., respectively, reflects how the interaction between the potentially endless act of orienting oneself, and that of execution — can produce a quality of allure provided they emerge according to certain combinations.

It's useful to acknowledge that whether one's days are understood as wisely invested or otherwise, that in each case it's the habits woven from moment to moment which formulate the totality of a person across time. Whether what "should" be done presents itself as an object of communicable validity stands trivial next to whether one can perceive in themselves those brief intersections wherein periods of constancy substitute with those of affectable malleability, as it's in those transient pockets the trajectory of one's course is ripest for alteration. Not only does the absence of awareness concerning that particularity nurture the threat of unwitting stagnance, but so too the intractability of unplanned chaos.

To master what wake one generates in space-time is to know oneself the laboriously remediated perpetrator of what's opposite their most preferred effect — for the breaks in any pattern are unavoidable, and cause it to run counter to its ordinary momentum. The observation follows that it's those with the finest control over their patterns who experience most acutely the dissonance resultant from deviations in their intent. Turbulence in habit is arguably the mechanism responsible for maintaining some semblance of scale respecting the ratio of improvement to friction in any given domain. The salience of a missed mark grows in proportion with what focus that mark is attended.

Competently managing what fluctuation one undergoes while endeavoring to succeed when the condition of one's stakes appears high, is facilitated to the degree of detachment mustered *following* the revelation that such success might be feasibly attained. In some sense, the most unfortunate thing that can befall a person is a vast quantity of unanticipated wealth, for without having pursued a balance lying beyond the dramas of carnal transaction — the whorls of its ebb following any massive flow are liable to prove catastrophic. It's not without tribulation that's assimilated, however — the surfer only learns to bide their time in the water after squandering their energy over many an infantile crest, and to with all energy assail waves of promise after seeing so many break beyond the reach of their board.

Hardly are there moments in the composition of one's ideal future where even the immediate map forward is without a quantity of details so confounding upon close analysis that the destination and every conceivable route toward it aren't conscionably disregarded as completely ridiculous outside a tailored set of mental gymnastics fallible in themselves from the first proposition upon which they depend to be justifiably carried out. The difference between genius and insanity depends on whether one sees that the incessant drive toward anything is completely meaningless, or potentially afforded meaning after it forces the emergence of some secondary set of phenomena — though which constitutes which is interminably debatable. The reason courage is central to the human capacity for expansion is because the probability of exacting some specific outcome even with the most fervent attention is something like that of exacting the same from a fistful of pitched dice.

To follow a certain course, it's necessary to access the inspiration of one's idols sparingly — because otherwise it becomes stale, and what one's accomplished having used it to cultivate momentum will itself appear likewise. There's no magic in becoming a carbon-copy of one's role models, even though on paper it promises a simple, unchanging path to tread. Instead of fighting oneself where there's a difference in behavior compared to some personified ideal — perhaps it's wiser to simply recognize those points of failure without criticism, abiding the notion that their transformation is predicated on their acceptance. It's so in many cases — a willingness to release control is the catalyst for escaping some painful eddy of compulsive sabotage. By taking away one side of the reciprocal force driving the repetition of a behavior, i.e., the retrospective polemic one directs at themselves — the phenomenon as a system loses half its energy, becoming null without that equal opposite attitude it would normally employ as a launchpad for its manifestation.

To act without paying attention in full to what exactly one engages themselves with is the principal cause for self-inflicted behavioral entrapment. Knowing oneself to fail is merely the initial condition for initiating a mission of voluntary rectification — it's the time spent attending what unsavory cesspit one partakes of without pinching the nose or making a scene of one's intent to reject it which unskews its honest assessment; a thing's wounds are exacerbated when it's thrashed in punishment for what dysfunction they cause.

Gaining a vantage point from which to observe one's own idiosyncrasies requires at least the postponement of all attempts at making a point. The simplified term for describing such a state is "relaxation," but since it's quite played out, attempts to call for it often fall flat. Just the same way rising in a hot air balloon denotes one's separation from their normal bounds of operation, does what's being referred to remove one's body of concern from its regular habitat — facilitating a broader and less involved approach conducive to the type of consideration human beings, with their intrinsic vastness of perception, are best exalted by.

It's the reason certain individuals who are identifiably unwell give themselves away as such, honing in on subjects to the dogged perceptual exclusion of all else, floundering in observable ignorance to the animosity-absorbing elephant in the room — that any individuals' scope of apprehension is positively vanishing before the total cascade of ingestible data-points. That variety of ignorance renders one susceptible to relegation as too inadequately attuned to context to foster fluid communal integration. It's always a great mess to place too many chips on some angle of approach, for the same reason it would be to only eat peanuts, or only walk in one direction; what's of justifiable continuity must always only be regarded as a matter of secondary importance. If one mistakes the longevity properly possessed by background features upon which primary matters are contingent, as endogenous to the latter, the wick one burns giving focus to a candle, or the ink spent giving focus to a pen, or the love expressed giving focus to another — is all burnt, spent, and expressed in juxtaposition with the expectation of their permanence, and so one finds themselves trapped in a predicament where they're driving frantically to charge the battery in a vehicle whose alternator is broken, mistaking the necessity for its constant need of replacement with some fancifully ignorant rationalization, reinforcing persistence on their delusional crusade of wastefulness.

To reveal the missing factor which will grant the locus of one's attention its optimal function, it *must* be given space. One is then called to trust whatever that is to use the emptiness provided it as a catalyst for propagation, and beyond that merely to organize its milieu such that it would flourish beyond the parasitism of its opposite — as that would be provided the same degree of freedom from restrictive attendance, and thus the equivalent opportunity to flourish. Often, that possibility is precisely what inhibits one's abstinence from involvement for the sake of beneficial aeration; it's a gamble whether the space provided won't simply fill with unwanted variables — shackling further one's trust in their own character, polluting their prospective instrument of redemption via its exposure to rejected personal qualities antithetical to what qualify as presentable interests.

The acquisition of new experiences is what catalyzes the cultivation of wisdom sufficient to bolster stability. No amount of sheltered investigation can raise the ticker of retrospective satisfaction high enough for it to at any point register as a justifiable expenditure of time, because that method fails to generate the pressure consequential to an act demanding such violent personal perturbation that the scale meant to evaluate the bounds of one's development is shattered irreparably; its replacement only then imposing enough to warrant little less than an impermeable fastness of spirit to ascend — the operational leeway within the former parameters functionally delineating no more than a sandbox of possible outcomes thereby transformed into a spectrum of decisions to be made whose consequences are disregarded at nontrivial expense.

Decisions characterized at a minimum by gravity which, if ignored, would prove satisfactorily cataclysmic that an unbroken chain of conscious deliberation is invoked in the service of its circumvention, can only manifest as real when the object of desire would fall out of reach should one allow themselves the slightest deviation in trajectory; the narrow road is as such not because its bounds are externally enforced — but because those who travel it should expect to arrive somewhere quite specific. Indeed — it's feasible for the aimless to attend it, but not without the quantum of friction one's spirit demands in exchange for being subject to unexplained confinement. It's best, on such a path, to have as much of one's system as possible in tune with the implications of its culmination — else its simplicity, which may otherwise have been a source of gratitude, is likely to impress itself as insufferable.

It isn't until the fruit of one's patient persistence is destroyed that the world clarifies as a place wherein the sacred and the fragile are welded together. Since it is the beginnings of life when one wields the most chaos, it's intuitive to understand youthful volatility as a lavic river whose aftermath nurtures growth, but perhaps not to translate the entire analogical causality, in cogent terms, into the human domain. Though lava does not observably endure any pangs of regret after razing flora, and its propagative effects are attributed to chemical processes beyond and behind the veil of perceptible qualia — they can be conceptually extrapolated such that they manifest through people resultant of their intrinsic sensitivity to the throes of their own wanton destabilization.

Most are prone to settle into some generically comfortable rhythm of understanding when drawing such comparisons, which, based on their background, will either reduce the human experience to something quite sterile, inanimate, or otherwise subjectively oversimplified; or project the dramas of reality as personally undergone onto what it contains — heedlessly stripping the apparently mundane from any pebble and exalting it to the status of high sentience, stumbling into what could be considered objective oversimplification. *Neither method is efficacious enough to constitute an airtight illustration that what's being connected has any business being connected at all.* Oddly enough, the impossibility of quantifying that necessity for connection on one side of the coin is likely to render it justifiable on the other; in an enormous way, this is the fundamental dichotomy between spirituality and science. To elucidate the world in a manner which honors the thirst for meaning — dealing with the complexities of physical incarnation as a distasteful side-effect; or to present it as an endless, interlocking series of arbitrary phenomena — relegating emotional vicissitudes to the subcategory of inane afterthought. As either approach is rejected, the other interlopes into one's experience like a neglected cousin cast down from the cosmic blueprint to tickle one out of stasis.

It's just as ridiculous to attempt to connect with another by aimlessly classifying things in the environment as it is to buy into the stock market based on a general feeling of excited optimism, but somehow the appropriate solutions to either of these problems share no margin that if crossed reveals the "correctness" of the means employed with anything remotely approximating universality — even that exhibition of "ridiculousness" relies heavily on reciprocal acceptance of what's essentially an improvised candidate for consensus. Perhaps the reason so much contention surrounds the notion of "common sense" is because the first half of that phrase is too often uttered with the intent to convey frequency, when in reality what it means is "common" in the sense that the existence of the "sense" in question is predicated on mutual agreement. With larger and larger local populations, or an expanding group of friends — the complexity involved with including contrary notions of what's sensible often finds resolution in the minting of some third precept designed exclusively for that purpose, whose constitution is as the offspring of the two initially in conflict.

This process is what denotes the progression of cultural amalgamation, and represents a sort of grafting action which although ultimately provisional and necessitating perpetual maintenance — appears to be the optimal means by which a functioning model of the universe is adapted across scale. The difficulty with manually expediting this process is that it depends entirely on the willingness of the two masses to encounter the unknown — and it isn't merely that there would be new frontiers to include on one's cognitive map, but the likelihood of imposed revisions whose acceptance would instantly call the validity of one's legend for the entire landscape into question. The endeavor of fluidly interlacing two modes of reasoning which only function locally actually depends on the honesty of the outlier to embody the essence of what makes them present as alien, because instead of leaking obtrusively from someone otherwise straining to exhibit seamless deference — it's as though the lingering atmosphere of their locality composes a radius around them, engendering an intersection where there's flexibility in the cultural rules, while still remaining subordinate to those principal in the region. It takes a tremendous amount of both courage, and sensitivity, to execute this effectively.

Without open discussion surrounding the prospect of culturally irreconcilable differences, it's a wonder their emergence doesn't always prompt immediate turbulence. The case could, of course, be that it does, only it's absorbed into the greater tendency to stoically shoulder such disturbances, saving any expression of discontent for some juncture where it might be released without impediment — multiplying the cycle of abrasion's total momentum in exchange for the circumvention of immediate discomfort. For example: it's a point of immense curiosity (and therefore debate) where the line is drawn between those phenomena one ascribes as causally predicated or not on one's own actions.

From one perspective, the individual is but a single instance of uncountable nodes gyrating in synchrony — far from capable of anything contrary to the greater currents wherein they're embedded, to the point that even their assessment of their own agency could be said to be outside their sphere of influence. It's notable, however, that a uniform emergence of disdain arises in those who hold such perspectives when they're accused of leveraging a viewpoint they not only would disagree they've the capacity to honestly and originally take on, but laud as though their voices could do anything but fall on the deaf, essentially mindless ears of whomever they're trying to sway — according to their own logic. From another, as the sole nexus wherein each experience is processed and interpreted, it is not only one's exclusive responsibility to respond to all stimuli in a manner which falls in perfect accordance with their personal philosophy, but completely inexcusable for anyone to expend energy so much as insinuating that the contrary could be the case. It's notable, however, that unless there was some modicum of unconscious influence working outside one's perceptual breadth, there would be no foundation upon which to conceptualize the world, and thus no means by which to establish even the most rudimentary suppositions — i.e., one's every intent is infected with the blind faith intrinsic to walking through a world whose rules are devised by its progenitors.

Notice how the approaches are opposed on no more than a superficial basis, as it's both impossible to function rationally without admitting possession of *at least* one's steering wheel while careening through creation — and similarly impossible to proceed without treading upon a past whose development had virtually nothing to do with oneself. If that point is never verbally conjured between two who occupy opposing sides of the relevant spectrum, it's less than feasible for the total quantity of confusion between them to do anything save expand as each spins up the other's respective resistance to compromise.

Shying away from the prospect of embodying stupidity is little more than a misunderstanding of the cockeyed glare aimed at one when they utter something oblique to another's item of presently elected pertinence. For as absolute as that other might evince their thoughts to be — notice if that were truly the case there would be no need to shoot any flavor of emotionally charged glance anywhere. Language as an instrument chips selectively at the infinite potential silence is pregnant with — akin to a sculptor's chisel. To surface on the interior of another's lexiconic chamber they've spent their life excavating without any show of recognition for what work in progress has just been intruded on — is like two mute painters before an infinite canvas forced to reconcile a brush stroke laid by one in the negative space the other understood as part of their piece. There's no justification to consider it any more offensive than an innocent accident — it's just quite disconcerting. That being said, each operates with the foresight that those roles could be laid in any configuration upon anyone at any moment, and consents to that reality the instant they begin whittling at the great shared carnal substrate with what they choose to say.

To argue about speech, there is always the confounding centrality to contend with, that it's the distance between the *meaning* behind words, and the words themselves — which incites struggle. *The words themselves* are discussed as though they've skin in the game, as though they're the very locus of value, because they're totally ubiquitous as the primary brokers of meaning; words are of commodities as dollars — so though purely representative, they stand in for stuff of sustenance consistently enough to become regularly confused with it. It is very tricky to convey a retooling of language which successfully bonds contrasting attitudes such that they're superimposed with enough stability to be reused without the accompaniment of an unwieldy quantity of rectificatory context. This is hardly surprising granted it's typical to undergo a casual conversation wherein the most elementary takes are challenged adequately to prompt some subsequent introspective grapple.

15

COMMUNICATION, RESOLVE

A person cannot draw the line demarcating themselves where they would their conclusions generally, because the latter would extend infinitely past the deepest depths and the highest heights of conceivable intricacy — resulting in a character divorced on all fronts from any concrete impression, and therefore, ironically, likenable to the shifty sort liable to strike the senses so fraudulently as to be revolting. It's arguable that the personality is something manifesting at the exact point one chooses to lie — an expression of attachment emanating from the elementally transient. Could it be that the only way to embrace authenticity is to abandon the prospect?

Or perhaps one should take infallible authenticity as granted in everyone, but their attempts to deliberately reveal themselves — for hopelessly flawed. Or perhaps it's that what manifests to the self as a core of intent exclusive to one's physicality — the conscience, per se, is not more than another of its features, the relationship between the two constituting no mystery at all, but simply organized to present what would among humans be referred to as an existential drama in precisely the same manner that birds present whatever it is they do to one another in the form of chirping; the multitude of tongues spoken throughout the world no more and no less consequentially differentiated than each avian call; the small throat sounds comprising the edifice of language no more and no less comparable than to skin — the most outwardly apprehendable layer of acoustic and light waves, respectively.

The entire question of what comprises intentional communication is somewhat like inquiring whether a window is part of a wall. The quality of their relationship is taken for granted, but upon closer inspection, the associated film of certainty is purged rather quickly. A window cannot be removed from a wall without disrupting the latter's integrity to the same degree as if it had a rectangular gash cleaved anywhere else on its surface, though visibly such a removal would be virtually indistinguishable from a window. Windows are ethereal unto themselves, but relate to walls in such a way that despite their perceptible contrast, the hierarchy of necessity between the two is virtually indeterminate — making it positively tortuous to distinguish where either ends and the other begins.

Communication is similarly indifferentiable from the other features employed to maintain homeostasis in the sense that it's seamlessly integrated with the greater structure of physical phenomena, but functions to such distinct ends that it more closely resembles most people's idea of magic than the fleshy, laryngeal oscillation it'd be acceptably described to a phenomenologist as. Even with *that* being the case, the question must be begged of whether on its account everything a person does that isn't normally *considered* communicative — is? Does not the fact that a window cannot exist without a wall mean every wall within which there's a window, is, for all intents and purposes, itself *essentially* a window? Would it truly be worth incarnating if it were not for the means to commune with other entities, reveling in mutual revelation for decades and centuries and millennia? The very blood which energizes worldly interaction is exactly that: *inter*-action; isn't it so that it permeates all the minutest experiential tangents — just as the heart diverges into innumerable capillaries?

The other similarity between windows and communication is that they both trade the ease of establishing clarity for a degree of exposure. Though the lot of what one plans to transmit can be selectively mediated using tools like scrupulous word choice and inflection — for those skilled at reading into context, humans leak an astonishing amount of information based on no more than the subtleties of their relationships to their environments. People are choiceless to be perceived — an otherwise perfectly reclusive hermit sighted even once is immediately vulnerable to interpretation. It might be reasoned there's nothing genuinely conveyed if the one from whom information is being gleaned isn't voluntarily participating in the exchange, but since the opposite party's narrative composes half the picture even in a mutually sanctioned situation, electing to forfeit that coin flip dictating success in getting one's share of their own impact across with an agreeable measure of accuracy means only that the outcome is left to a fate of greater improbability — not somehow likely to collapse into something appreciable.

The impasse of miscommunication is chargeable to the irreplicable novelty of personal experience complexifying the network of shareable data points every time a conversation transpires — drastically outpacing any individual's advancement toward linguistic mastery. It's interesting to consider whether language as a system could be regarded inherently flawed on account of this, because the implication is that it effectively conjures a hydra for each problem it solves. It should be noted as well that language in this context, though referred to through the lens of conversation — is meant as a stand-in for all manners by which the cogent transference of human sensation is striven after.

There are modes of expression whose lack of semantic fungibility is supposed to be granted, but the line past which that's the case isn't clear-cut. All are apt at intervals to take what's purposely presented as concrete for abstract, and vice versa. It isn't only as though the shared reality everyone walks through seems to increasingly dissolve into an amorphous stew of potential for each additional person speaking their mind, but that with that as the case, those categories most optimally employed to sort the matter in solitude are largely up in the air as well. It's those countless, varying refractions a thing undergoes as it passes through people on the way to oneself which fleshes out its relevance. Humans trust one another to reciprocally solidify their descriptions of what's going on, weaving communicable reality using an appreciation for the total lot of established suppositions — combined with credence for what conclusions that mass, digested, elicits from oneself.

When asked to explain something in a different way, the immediate grapple invoked within is predicated on a feeling of loss from being prompted to abandon an entire series of logical connections at the behest of someone who's simply unfamiliar with them. The initial instinct might be to recapitulate the whole litany of precursory information framing whatever was presented — but it's not much of a leap to assess that task about half as reasonably undertaken than starting from scratch with the space just prior to that other's limits of conceptual cooperation as a launchpad.

With that said, it's no trivial feat remaining true to the essence of the original notion while altering its phrasing to fit comfortably in range of another's grasp — especially when it's almost guaranteed those new terms will be imbued with presuppositions of their own, necessitating an additional tier of internal reconciliation before the new explanation can be comfortably deployed. That's to say one is obliged, when asked to overhaul some position for clarity's sake, not only to assume a stance appropriate to frictionlessly integrate with the entreating party's purview of reasoning — but to simultaneously shoulder the onus of solitarily translating that which one suspects that other would find intelligible, back into what personally rings true. It's for this reason all masterful professors are also masterful analogists — the ability to spin a thing several different ways is paramount to proficiency in compelling a room to abjure its confusion. It is, in addition, the ultimate means to hone one's own understanding, for it transforms what was once a particular subject into something accessible from a multitude of angles, augmenting not just its utility, but the efficiency with which it can be summoned under a variety of circumstances.

Though influenced by the respective willingness of both parties, imparting information is a mission quite on the order of achieving orgasm; there are times when it inexplicably ensues from an otherwise perplexing or unengaging state of affairs — and also from those wherein one may have otherwise wished to postpone or avoid it altogether. It seems, generally, to go without question that having more information is always better — but it's far from difficult to retrospectively cherry-pick units of knowledge which if never initially acquired would have permitted some series of events to ostensibly unfold much smoother. Superficially, this reads as a reasonable enough assessment — after all, it's all too real how lost one can become absorbing data in such a manner that if it were water would make one seem as though they intended to single-handedly imbibe the ocean.

But what of time's march, which precludes certainty of whether where one treads principally concerned with the imperative of safety isn't but a path tracing about just what opportunities would prove genuine boons? One reaches an impasse wishing away the past not because it's immutable, *for although wishing is the wrong approach, just about anything can be favorably recontextualized provided diligence is exercised in the present* — but because at some point that wish will directly conflict with interests one possessed preceding the problematic event in question which only could have been altered resultant to that, or some other comparable event. If something goes so wrong one questions their sanity beyond the tail end of it, the relevant implication is not that things would've, should've, and could've gone better if it would simply have had the decency not to transpire — but that if it hadn't happened there would still be an extra insane character waltzing mindlessly across the Earth's surface, passively influencing others to conduct themselves likewise.

When comparing the several distinct versions of oneself emerging across time, the moments therein possessed of the most change will be seen to partition them, and abide a twofold pattern — often qualitatively mistaken in their entirety as either of their halves. The experience of intense change is neatly divisible into event and response; they're confused because what emotions emerge in tandem with a given occurrence can tend to indiscriminately permeate one's field of perception, which would otherwise include the fissure splitting them. I.e., agency in responding can seem a vague notion with one's judgement clouded by a sudden ingress of volatility; this doesn't mean one stands inculpable for its clarification and subsequent exercise.

One is stuck when they believe their energy expenditure to be fruitless. Since all efforts directly translate to an alteration in the environment, however, it's little more than a comforting illusion to believe oneself in any respect exempt from the responsibility of making an impact on account of plain impotence. There is often the misunderstanding that a hammer swung earnestly through open air without striking a solid surface does not accomplish anything — when in fact the mounting internal perturbation caused precisely by that apparent absence of effect makes colossal waves within oneself; the mistake is in refusing to acknowledge oneself as part of the environment. Hard work is touted as an ultimate virtue because as long as there's genuine effort, there's genuine development. If one insists on exclusively abiding external markers of growth, they'll find an excuse related to their own inabilities readily at hand — it's the only sensible conclusion if they've not been familiarized with pain and confusion as signs of weakness and stupidity leaving the body, respectively.

The silent battles fought each day are far from inconsequential — least of all when they feel insurmountable. To rise in defiance of odds which make "overwhelming" sound like a dismal understatement is the first spark of a *readiness to molt* — and ensures maximum efficiency as one navigates toward their goals, because the associated degree of fear serves to indicate their proximity to physiological impossibility and/or irremediable ostracism, the two working together to spell the only legitimate boundary before which the resolve to use one's capacities will cause them to forge forth in an unbroken skyward trajectory. In other words, the ones who fear running out of gas most acutely are those likely to actually use the lot of the tank. If there's time and energy enough to be concerned with what will constitute the leg of one's mission following that which is presently at hand — the expectation of its yield is most sensibly assimilated into that of the initial endeavor, and the gravity of the latter upscaled to accommodate it.

When one shoulders a problem beyond the border delineating what they find themselves able to gainfully resolve on a consistent basis, they skulk through the limbo of latent creativity. It is the frontier where hope and despair wear one and the same skin, genius and idiocy are indistinguishable, and the projectable return on investment of slamming one's head against the wall in a fervent bid to jostle anything quantifiable from the grey is drawn parallel with that of wandering aimlessly through a field of flowers. It's the kind of place requiring one to submit to their intuition in order to escape, because what emotions dominate while stumbling through it, are reflected in all it contains.

Despite any virtues one might righteously insist they're championing — nothing in that domain is to be gained while it's patrolled with the belief one's engaged in some tense struggle whose subsequent frustration is expected to do anything save propagate itself. Insisting on a particular type of resolution only locks one into a recursive bout with the specter of whatever issue it might have sufficed to resolve — as making assumptions in a creative context is an act of creation itself, and as relates to the greater objective, merely spawns devils in addition to that one's tasked themselves to slay, who if entertained will effortlessly stall one so the central necessity can never be addressed. When handling new difficulties, one only needs their heading, their patience, and their bearing as they come across novel complexity — creating friction under such conditions is like cursing at locals for giving directions in the local language. That being said, during the creative process, it's important not to conceptualize whatever's necessarily redacted after having acted from a place of mad, racing confusion, as the kind of mistake hopelessly nullifying the solution to a math equation.

If one imagines the road to completion including every scratched-out, painted-over, reassessed feature — it's clear in retrospect that if one were to have given up on account of any of them, no amount of perfectly executed work thereto would be compensation enough to bring the project to its completion. The function of a mistake is a funny thing; before the moment they're all accounted for and systematically wiped from perception, they're the loathsome epitome of hindrance — only thereafter does their quality completely invert, and crystallize into impermeable armor in whose face challenges lesser than those from which it's composed are laughably ineffectual.

Regarding the nature of advancement in a self-directed atmosphere versus that within a prescribed system, the former holds more potential overall, while the latter provides stability combined with an amount of external accountability, permitting one to track their development relative to communally sanctioned milestones — though those are only really useful if one flies blind to the positive increments in their own competence, which they'll anyway find recommended as most wisely attended in search of fulfillment should they openly fixate on competition to the detriment of their craft. The benefit of undelegated responsibility is it forces the prioritization of discipline in ways which generate tangible personal returns. One is punished with a swiftness bordering instantaneous when they alone shoulder the repercussive brunt of every misstep they make — it is a thankless task to secure oneself a curated future until its survival value proves definite enough that it can stand fast as an example for others.

It's an extremely high-risk high-reward activity to pursue such a path, because the lack of credibility prior to the greater acknowledgment of its validity distills at that transitive juncture into the novelty serving to propel it into mass appreciation. That happens because although there's the promise of a significant quantum of safety inherent to options whose history vets them as prudent, most find the prospect of identifying with some shiny, elite new way of being, without the danger of eating shit while testing its components in development — positively delicious. The nuances of that reality also explain why a friend or close acquaintance might confer support in confidence for one's personal investment into a fresh idea, but among crowds feign ignorance, or even denounce it as foolish; the immediate problem of being regarded a fool by association aches indefinitely, but is quelled provided the pioneer in question throws in the towel — thusly are honor as a friend and the potential status as an early investor traded for momentary comfort and the maintenance of outward cultural conformity.

One might argue not only that there are instances where every party in question fares better with the absence of a single soul's thirst for disruptive innovation, and maybe even that that inference functions as a respectable baseline from which to operate — although it's impossible to ascertain whether it's ever warranted, because it itself is a contributing factor in whether the ambition falls through. Those seeking to thrive on their own terms should avoid placing an excess of stock in the opinions of their peers; it's unwise to expect support when there's a decent likelihood it's hollow on account not only of their total lack of skin in the game, but also because one's voluntary engagement with such an unforgiving trial offers little in the way of anyone else's foreseeable benefit (it's liable to cause in them a comparably minor version of the dismay experienced upon uncovering another's suicidal ideations) — meaning until it's matured to the point of working as a means to consistently procure sustenance, the whole enterprise, whether one likes it or not, is tainted with a sort of hazardous ambiance wherever it's presented. Getting into a rhythm of replacing credence for others' expressed opinions with inanimate criteria is perhaps the trickiest and most powerful internal edit one can make to maintain a sane, consistent basis from which to foster independent cultivation. It's without, initially, the dopaminergic flood so easily acquired indulging in validation from one's peers — but its equal dearth of volatility means success in heeding it to the exclusion of outside influence facilitates access to a reward system whose activation obliges guidelines mapping directly onto quantifiable progress, unbinding the application of one's faculties from what erraticism pollutes the default context of socially derivable validation.

One can only appeal to those masses who possess half the power to render one successful by doggedly abiding their own principles during their work. If so much as the *predilections* of any others are consciously calculated — the integrity of the endeavor falls short. Each person is the perfect nexus of everything they encounter, and so by extension, the connections one hosts represent their absolute maximum range of effect. To place gravity on any fraction, i.e., to siphon anything less than the totality of one's experience into the final elixir — indicates a lack of sincerity in their need to follow their own way, and subsequently that they've chosen to suffer the weight of that responsibility in vain. It should take no more effort to consciously arrive at the next step than it does to absorb the colors of a sunset. That is to say, one cripples themselves forcing a choice between however many options — the correct answer is borne of such a widely comprehensive selection of factors that it *materializes before one* infinitely moreso than it's opted for.

It might be reasoned that such a phenomenon would be functionally indifferentiable from a symptom of confirmation bias, but its nature is such that it cancels out preferential and disparaging arguments alike — like a perfectly straight line discovered between two points while one evaluates the viability of numerous paths. The impasse of whether a thing should be taken seriously when it's without any lineage of explicable rationality can make it extremely troubling for one to convey the importance of some such intuitively originated intent, because as opposed to in those conversations shared between people unfamiliar with their own purest interests, having unwittingly cast them into the subdomain of veiled luxury — the typical justificatory niceties are expendable without one's aspirations constrained to an unspoken consensual framework wherein each competes to assure themselves of their own sensibility via incessant comparison. One's best and worst impressions pending the receipt of any nontechnical criticism are liable to span from brusque to outright arrogant exposed to such spheres — palpable dissonance is engendered where one's convictions dispassionately cross lines before which another unquestioningly yields, because as long as the others in that other's environment appear to be observing the same limits, the ease characterizing their affairs can continue to be comfortably taken for granted. If one seeks to develop themselves without the overbearing parameters endemic to a prefabricated pathway visibly buckling under its own prevalence — all that's needed is a friend who's on a similar track, or better yet a personal mentor whose selection is predicated on no more than that they strike one as unnervingly capable.

16

COMPULSION, SENSITIVITY

T he word "expect" is used to denote a strong intimation that something *will* happen, and occupies the blacklist of terms which are insidiously misconstrued on a regular basis. Mostly that's due to its erroneous, implicit synonymization with the phrase "strongly hope" — suggestively augmenting the probability of one's favored outcome to the exclusion of others, as though it would be in violation of some natural law for anything contrary to manifest. Consistently weaponizing language this way is a surefire means to condition others into compliance against their better judgment — especially if they're trusting.

It's safe to have high hopes and measured expectations, and to communicate all of the above *as clearly as humanly manageable*. A well-intentioned confession of "expectation" without anything concrete enough to communicably justify it is poisonous and misleading; it's like confidently confirming a clear shot as a spotter while blindfolded. More frequently than not, such situations are purely unintentional. One who doesn't understand the division between their calculations and their sentiments will rampantly mislead those they love as a standard, simply because they're accustomed to buffering every instance of anxiety with emotionally charged recourse, rendering them not only incapable of effectively rectifying themselves, or even of delineating what constitutes a legitimate problem on anything steadier than a timescale varying in total subordination to their emergent feelings — but also of consciously segregating their advice from what's identifiably anything more than thoughtless manipulation.

It's extremely powerful to have one's feelings working in tandem with their rationality, but if that latter foundation is missing — all bets placed are dubious, because they're governed by what's so intrinsically volatile that the likelihood they'll independently map to anything the future holds is reduced to random. There's the additional factor, as corresponds in the market, that the qualitative background of a situation is colored by those of every gamble made therein — the *instant* they're made. With a broad enough history of unabashed reactivity, unpredictability falls in line with rational expectations not because it's predestined, but because to steadily nurture any habit is to reinforce its dominion over oneself — one's soul signed away via a contract they themselves are burdened to draft.

Whether such a contract can be said to possess the same finality as one concerning separate entities is not quite so straightforward as declaring it null on account of its parties occupying the same individual, and by extension operating at the behest of the same desire. It could be said that as a contingency for preventing such a simple breach — the traditional, lightweight bindings of ink on paper typically serving to represent agreement are replaced in these cases with the necessity to undergo an amount of discomfort as would've been experienced without the habit replacing it. That is to say, it forces one to struggle while returning to a baseline which when finally attained will be experienced as significantly more effortful to maintain than when it was previously in reach, perhaps until one breaks even with the quantity of time spent divorced from it. Note particularly that to initiate the bond, the victim must voluntarily offer the pathology permission and encouragement for it to build sufficient momentum that it carries forth on its own in the same manner as a regular affliction.

The poignance of this impasse has to do with the fact that when the relationship to the tendency is forged, those in question may not be cognizant of the greater social structure dictating which are wisely embodied — and so take it on unwittingly. Or, in fact, it may be of sincere utility under what circumstances it's initiated, but gradually shifts out of bounds *following* its complete assimilation into the personality. Another perspective is that no system of behavior should be shunned or automatically subjected to backlash, total autonomy being the highest cultural aspiration — and there are many more.

If one wishes to credibly foster a more generalized appreciation for *any* of these viewpoints, however — the matter of re-establishing control over one's person *must* take precedence over their advocation. Firstly this is because the few willing to spare their condolences in response to the presentation of such observations are themselves likely prey to comparable compulsions — and so are as cellmates obliged to corroborate one's justificatory narratives in order to render the shared space altogether more bearable. Maybe not so much secondly, but the perhaps not immediately evident argument stemming directly from that last is that nobody in their right mind takes the shrill indignance emanating from a manhole below which the catacombs of the societally vexed echo with less than a mass of salt sufficient to cure an entire whale. So — assuming one's pried themselves from the grips of some habit responsible for turning the majority of its hosts into a statistic, the beginnings of an inkling of an intimation of a comprehensively satisfactory approach in dealing with instances of *that specific hangup* can be entertained. The following dialectic isolates sensitivity as its subject, for that virtue, in the presently discussed and in all other domains, stands at the pinnacle of those instruments vital in honing the astuteness of one's considerations:

Sensitivity is the capacity to register salience throughout the various levels and intricacies of a thing; how must one's relationship to the matter in question be adjusted to afford maximal sensitivity to it? With sensitivity posing as the objective, the first basic paradox one encounters surrounds the question of whether it's blunted or amplified by relevant experience. Should one seek to sensitize themselves by holding excessive stimuli at bay, will they not become counterproductively habituated to shutting out exactly what of the world they intend to unveil? If one should seek to consistently expose themselves in a bid for the acquisition of greater knowledge, do they not anesthetize themselves to its nuances? Is not the notion of "being able to handle" greater quantities of information the same thing as being calloused, i.e. — desensitized? What is basically the difference between two people who feel the same thing, and evince comparatively disproportionate reactions? The plainest answer seems to be that by default they can't be feeling the same thing — but then that relegates the entire discussion of sensitivity vs a lack thereof to that between weakness and strength, fundamentally. Or would it? A powerlifter and an average person arguably possess the same range of sensitivity to heft, but the former's will begin and end at a substantially higher weight than the latter. So how could one simultaneously increase the lower and upper limits of their sensitivity to manageably imbibe the theoretical maximum load of data? It seems as though it would be like asking someone to sprint and sit still at the same time.

Indeed it would be; the only solution is to employ a group of individuals with varying perspectives, and work toward establishing a body of knowledge which as many of that group as possible are, as a rule, *partially* satisfied with. This will fall apart if where the extreme ranges of each overlap are discussed as though the contrast among the interpretations is appalling, however. That is to say, the aforementioned model of *relative* sensitivity to phenomena must be communally acknowledged. If anything is to be suggested for *the individual* as relates to the maximization of sensitivity, then it's to detach one's identity both from what one finds overwhelming, and underwhelming — and to seek companionship and attempt to harbor sincerely involved discourse with those who possess apparently inverse angles on reality and its contents.

With that established, it may be worthwhile to differentiate sensitivity from expertise, for despite the earlier illustration that the former is diametrically opposed to one's familiarization with some specific sphere — the enormous value in practice, which could be mistaken as nonexistent in light of that, is inextricably bound to the latter. In essence, they're of equal and opposite importance. Sensitivity is crucial in areas requiring a gentle appreciation for the many facets of what one must acknowledge as new to them — ultimately including every situation possessed of dynamism adequate to jostle one's convictions concerning that situation into an ever more balanced distribution across the lot of common perspectives relating to it. It is the orienting mode, so to speak, and functions both as the honed edge of what's being referred to as expertise, as well as the principal fail-safe at hand in lands uncharted. Expertise is where one's regular attendance to a finite selection of useful information provides a vantage point overlooking territory the majority of a given population would consider immense to the point of inscrutability in its novelty.

The relationship between expertise and sensitivity evolves over time the same way as the relationship of a home and/or workplace to its surroundings. The density of familiarity is necessarily greatest immediately outside the coordinates whereupon some pursuit can be reliably engaged without interruption, and dissipates therefrom gradually. University campuses are perhaps the most fitting examples of this — their easy character beyond their libraries and their lecture halls as such precisely to facilitate protected entry into the complex series of intellectual caverns they harbor. Notice too their soft jurisdiction will often extend into surrounding college towns — the partition between their internal culture, and what's outside, permeating deep into the localities to which they're central. On the other end of the scale, the extent of one's necessary expertise might inhabit no more than a set of equipment dense enough to fit in the confines of a backpack and be taken around the world.

The point is that those areas within which one finds themselves complemented are always sandwiched between an inner and outer zone of irregularity, and are unwisely lauded as superior to others when in light of more than the demands of a single person — they're only evaluable in terms of size. The inner zone of irregularity is of remarkable depth, and the object of calculated deliberation; the outer is the whole expanse of the outside world, and though is on the whole much more diverse in the litany of complexities it presents as opposed to the range wherein one is explicitly comfortable, is usually also tamed to the degree that it's more or less hitchlessly navigated by the general public. As one secures increasingly greater stability in their specific position, the value in what they've to share becomes unintelligible beyond the circle of those who've adopted their same domain of proficiency — i.e., unless possessed of communication skills rivaling one's skill in their specialty, one's friends are likely to be disproportionately reflective of their society vocationally. The inverse phenomenon, regarding those who're content with tending to a shallower scope of affinity, open themselves to a wide mass of collective appreciability in exchange for the ever-present need to shift about in search of pockets suitable for professional exploitation. Consider the axis between them marked at opposing ends by a pure mathematician and a travel photographer.

17

SHOOTING STRAIGHT

I s it sensible to reward oneself? Ostensibly, the primary benefit of a reward is that it's rendered at another's expense — a glorified form of compensation, in essence. There are arguably two fatally detrimental consequences in doing so. The first is that one cannot conscionably spin the incentivizing factor of a reward as preserved while relieving oneself of the means necessarily expended on its procurement — it would be like trying to reap energy from a power strip plugged into itself. The second is that as one acclimates to practicing it, they prematurely cap their capacity to register the full gravity of a legitimate reward — jeopardizing the only mechanism by which the consensual optimization of behavior between two or more entities can functionally take place.

So — not only does rewarding oneself conceptually bastardize the integrity of one's justification for organic reciprocity, but by some twisted miracle of impatience-induced idiocy, has one *pay upfront* for its destruction. Even if the payoff is of indeterminate size and form, taking an immediate loss entailing no investment at all instantly involves infinitely more risk than merely exercising the faith necessary to hold out for it. This assumes, of course, that one operates in voluntary accordance with a ruleset whose prerequisites for success are both definite, and extrinsically defined.

What bounds one uses to mentally separate the endogenous responses of the system they perceive themselves to be engaged with from autonomous commands they impose from a point of view external to it, and in an ultimately arbitrary relation to its state, need to be specified, because it isn't always the case that another party bestows the relevant set of consequences when dealing in the prescribed confines of a particular situation. E.g., the acquisition of a car adjusts one's baseline of mobility the same way a newfound consistency in exercising adjusts one's baseline of caloric expenditure; whether whether one travels or eats more in response are viably regarded as proper rewards intrinsic to those changes, is at the complete discretion of the individual.

Really though, it's something of a luxury to live with unquestioned access to a predetermined framework which automatically spells out terms of accomplishment without one's intervention. It permits the unadulterated streamlining of focus much the same way as bowling lane bumpers. It's arguable there's a complete absence of dignity in shamelessly touting one's prowess under such conditions, but it's also true that without conceding to some such set of parameters — the prospect of gainfully orienting oneself in the world is literally hopeless. After all, the principles at play in the implementation of advantageous simplifications are the same as what are used to construct a bowling lane in the first place. A level floor and a standard system of points and a socially sanctioned setting developed for the express purpose of facilitating bowling — would otherwise be deservedly equated to cheap conveniences. Differentiating overengineered reward structures from indispensably foundational regulations boils entirely down to the question of how people determine *what it is they deserve.*

Following from the idea that there's no operable frame which doesn't basically work as a set of blinkers, since the context of any pursuit is quite promptly revealable as suspended within a series of infinitely nested justifications, *all facets of an ecosystem being not only totally interdependent, but manifesting in an incalculably faceted universe, and so dependent too on each of its minute finitudes* — there's the peculiar complication that the most oppositional reasons for why certain modes of being should take precedence *owe one another* what solid ground they've to support their respective arguments, and pointedly more so than those oblique in relation. Any position presented as innately superior will unfailingly paint its opposite as innately inferior, and in so doing establish a totally irrational yet ideologically impregnable position — held together with perfect confidence by nothing more than the insistence of polar difference. Which end of an argument one finds themselves on has nothing at all to do with the object of the argument itself, because in the same manner as a magnet — the factor determining whether an individual is attracted to a side of it versus repelled is simply which of *their* sides is frontal as they draw near.

What determines physical magnetism is no more than that all the electrons in a thing spin in the same direction, i.e. — where there appears to be an item of fundamentally visceral division, *it* is completely uniform, and those sucked into alignment with either of its ends confound the force screwing them down to it with some superstitious sacredness inherent to the thing itself. The reason it's difficult for people to flip their perspectives once they're locked into such an instance is the same as why its difficult to pry a chunk of iron off of a lodestone — but assuming it were done, it would be just as liable to reattach itself in the completely inverse orientation. This is why instead of directly refuting the validity of some perspective, a centered or disengaged person will appear to reserve themselves from comment. Once one declares that the possibility of becoming forcibly yet arbitrarily fixated on something is distasteful, they're prone, if anything, to invalidate the entire topic — deeming it unworthy of discussion.

This, however, is merely another expression of unwittingly polarized behavior. A human being's only constant, i.e., the quality which makes them just the same as all of what they're susceptible to being magnetized by, is the fact that they deteriorate over time. The very pursuit of avoiding attachment is faulty, because it betrays a desire to make something specific of oneself prior to death. All that's accomplished in the denial of that vulnerability is one's binding by the nape (and thus their blindness) to the publicly observable vehemence endemic to every peon vainly insisting their fixations are nothing less than universally impactful. To claim possession of infallible detachment is to argue one's invincibility with a self-inflicted killshot, the absence of gravity by exploding on impact from the fall off of a fourteen-story building, or the inanity of weapons while standing unarmed before what would elsewise be a perfect enfilade of lethally hostile combatants; the fact one deems it mentionable is the very mechanism by which its falsity is demonstrated.

Right — so the entire thing is woven together such that suicide and petulance basically constitute the sum of one's options outside frankly attending to, and admitting one's place within, the boundless lattice of transactional tension, wherever that may be. The importance of which part of that lattice one finds themselves abiding cannot be undervalued just because the style of its organization is mirrored throughout the rest of the world — this is like dismissing the first birthday of one's only child or an enrapturing piece of music because "it's all just a lot of atoms." Probably the most operable way to frame one's position, with all its perks and all its tribulations, is to depict it as one's personal domain of refinement — of which no other *could* be the master.

Clichéd and tautological as it may appear to encourage pride in oneself for its own sake, the absolute limit of calculable possibility falls entirely inside that class of phenomena whose contents are exclusively perceptible to the ones perceiving them, and so the game of disparagingly comparing oneself to others can be seen as moot not on account of one's lucky psychological penetration by a well-meant aphorism, but because what phantom futures one conjures fantasizing themselves as others can be conscionably looked upon as uncorrupted inspiration — perfectly viable as prospective avenues of personal development. There are no cookie-cutter solutions to those challenges which present themselves across the term of a lifetime — one can only trust what means they suspect themselves most wisely disposed in exercising at least compose the likely candidates for securing satisfaction.

One's nearest personal estimate of what's a waypoint is as reliably heeded as that in a video game by its own developers. Of course that example is perpetually iterable, because assuming one creates their direction begs in what service it's created, and from there it's either turtles all the way down, or there's a higher power whose effect results in each purpose's arisal as something akin to the crests of a thematic oscillation running throughout a given life, or set of lives. In any case, the most riveting colossi of meaning are utterly dependent on their cognitive inviolability for their grandiosity; whether their representation takes the form of deity, or self, or both, or neither, or anything — is largely peripheral.

Since every action's consequences play out with virtually no relation to their supposed precursory intentions — the style most fluidly aligned with any specific undertaking is to do it *for better or for worse*. The former half of that argument takes for granted that humans actually *aren't capable* of living by anything except their highest intentions. The human creature is either compelled to contribute to the greater system by what gain they understand they enjoy from it, or to destroy the greater system by what gain they understand they *could* enjoy from it, supposing it were differently organized. The basic premise is that a person attains their interpretation of themselves solely through the study of others (one or more others effectively instantiating a "greater system," which is pulled toward the manifestation of a pattern based off the actions of each individual within it), and so even in the case of an endeavor as disruptive and appalling as, say, *ethnic cleansing,* one's preservative instincts combined with the fact that there's an ultimately immovable core of empathy in everything anyone does, since, once again, the notion of oneself only exists as a reflection of what's external — compassion, which is the alleged basis of morality, must similarly be the basis of everything that happens as far as entities moving through abstracted models of themselves make anything happen at all. This is *not* a justification for horrific behavior — it serves to demonstrate that where there's ambiguity about what to be done, the solution has nothing to do with isolating and extricating any fatal flaw, but with retooling the density of each moment to foster as much diligence as is manageable. One might hope in so doing that they'd avoid a life tainted by the unforgivable shadow of mass casualties — the varied results of steadfastly sharpening oneself against the world being ample to round off what edges cause trifling ideological abrasion to stack masses of latent chaos before the temper's wick.

Better versus worse is basically an exercise in pitting colors against one another, because to live as a human is to have the internal rope used for that tug of war between good and evil constantly drawn even. Though it isn't possible to nerf one's ethical efficacy, what happens is it'll succumb to inertia before one's learned constraints, and if the ceaselessly testing quality of worldly tribulation stokes enough impatience, one becomes wont to abridge their chase after perfection, forcing its capture on a mortal time frame, and inciting friction where the responsibility of its eternal hunt reveals, like a dangerous stranger staring unblinking within a foot's distance, that brevity is not suitable in one's regard of it, and that in fact it should paint the forefront of one's awareness bright red until it's really actually dealt with — even and especially if that means until the junction whereupon death takes the reins of its long shift. Though grinding, and inevitable in its dearth of conclusiveness — it is not enough for that tug of war to be an equal fight; the line must be drawn taut, and attended with all attention, for it's the downward and inward forces of its competitors bracing the world against irremediable dissolution. Fervent consistency in whatever one chooses to do — that its rewards and its defects alike might be less painfully unveiled.

18

NERVE

Nervousness is simultaneously what objects to diving off the cliff, and what provides the launching force necessary to clear those jagged, shallow rocks lying past the water's edge. To be ashamed of nervousness is to be ashamed of one's own competence. If anything, one would be wise to acknowledge they ought to be intentionally wary if it's nowhere to be found in what to the logical faculties qualifies as a precipitous state of affairs — the line between bravery and stupidity is that between the unignorable thick of apprehension, and pompous indifference. This hardly means it's admirable to exist in a perpetual state of frenzied agitation — it's physiologically taxing over prolonged periods, and has absolutely no bearing on the success of an attempt if none are ever made on account of the discomfort it presents.

The behaviors considered candidates to be the keystone of one's legacy, once they're prioritized relative to death, stand as determinants up to which one engulfed by *that vexed condition peppered with incorrigibly fretful, nail-biting, pupil-dilating drunkenness prognosticating the inevitable encounter with a thing of substantial consequence, like an unwelcome messenger who offers only the foreboding ramblings of an imbecile, and ensures with naught but the look in their eyes they'd be liars to assure solace of any variety, who are reluctantly impelled to oblige one with their warnings by some long-dead specter of virtue once held, whose grave they all but spite outright for its lingering effect having cast them into a position so idiotically proximal to the scene of impending disaster* — may look. Three options present themselves when such psychic hazards are stumbled upon. One may pry ceaselessly into its implications, fruitlessly partaking of cortisol as though it were useful as anything more than a signal — and stall fatally. It's barely what could be called an option, but is nonetheless included for the frequency with which the human creature is apt to engage it as such.

The other two, then — are attack, and retreat. That aforementioned prioritization of worthy behaviors is called into play at this point, and though when vetted in solitudinous stability surely would've seemed to epitomize the impervious sanctity of idealism, will appear to the mind when that testing moment comes knocking as but a bit of ink scrawled across a tattered, crumpled scrap of paper, haphazardly taped to the mirror before which one stood long hours contemplating what it is to be. The contents of that tattered scrap *alone* need to determine what actions follow therefrom. It needs to stand as an iron bulwark against whatever madness vies to blight the instruments employed to forge it — for if in safety the tenets upon it were truly compared to the final drawing of the curtains and found to stand in their criticality alongside survival, it would be an affront to forfeit them at the behest of a threat even marginally lesser than death.

That may seem counterintuitive, because rationally, previous exposure to comparable catastrophe is warranted before judgment of how the actions in question fare in their importance relative to survival can with any accuracy be made — but the point is to nurture a pervasive willingness unsusceptible to wilting on contact with the *supposition* of

283

disaster, which when practiced in the face of lesser dragons can be unsheathed with increasingly laser-like efficiency. (Something about warriors and gardens and gardeners and wars.) A dependable set of principles is much more like a pearl than a shield, despite it functioning no differently from the latter when wielded in defense of a sudden and formidable quandary. Well — it's like a pearl insofar as a person is like a mollusk; it's cultivated internally in retaliation to deleterious foreign bodies, honed and shaped by one's repeated exposure to injury.

The mechanism by which one becomes something is an ironic sort of charade, because the fear of winding up keeping an indifferentiable ticky-tacky box, or other equivalent communally endorsed daymare, is a call to adventure which is either resentfully postponed, fumbled, and causes one to calcify belatedly — or boldly attended, and forces one face to face with the fact that there's an uncircumventable obligation to bed down into a rhythm of consistent effort while one's sensibilities are yet tainted by dependence-induced animosity for the system within which they reside, otherwise they'll never be able to effectively concoct themselves a future of appreciable novelty. To refuse the lesson in a petulant bid to perpetuate childhood is to harden asymmetrically into a chimeric mass of partial commitments. It is at once inadvisable to fight against the tide of time, and foolish to feel dejected in its shadow before having taken a few swings at it. Rebelling against the inevitability of crystallization is a surefire way to galvanize one's organization into a pleasant sort of crystal.

It should be noted there isn't exactly the kind of inevitability that if not submitted to through one's beliefs can be caught and held. Part of the reason for that is because to make a determination of any kind, it's first necessary to define what one's sure of. I.e., its nature, unless fleshed out in the light of those phenomena with which it cohabitates in space-time, can never be apprehended, and since it'll always butt up against the future (and by extension the totality of its contents), a comprehensive grasp of not only everything that has ever transpired, but everything that will ever transpire, is nonnegotiably prerequisite to assert with authority that something is incontrovertible. The reason the implication that that's not necessarily the case, or perhaps more accurately that its profundity can with effect be discarded, is appended providing one is possessed of sufficient certainty — is because there's the insane privilege as a human being to bulldoze through the matrix of available information in a way which makes it so criteria to confidently claim that a thing has come to pass can simply be hunted either until it's fulfilled, or indefinitely. Even death, ostensibly the most ubiquitously inevitable occurrence it's feasible to conjure with words, classically fails to put a stopper in the conviction of eternal life.

So far this has been made to sound as though what fates each lean into are upheld by little more than unscrupulous thinking, but it's not for nothing the means to cast even the weightiest dogmas aside in favor of one's own assessments is almost virginal in that when accepted as present in another, an irrefutable recognition emerges, the cosmic veto of unobstructed belief incites a grin coupled with the instinctual attraction of one's palm to their face — for the power of what's *considered* factual, like that which keeps a vampire from traversing the threshold of one's home, remains unmolested until it's deliberately relinquished. What *are* those items of impregnable knowledge that can compel people even into bloody conflict with one another? It seems on some level, though not nearly so tangible as that crimson nectar loosed by cold blades and hot lead — they've purchase on the soul such that they allow one to resolutely withstand the same carnal hardships they're leveraged to prevent.

Why is the power of being dead set on something of such overwhelming influence? Is the prospect of unguided psychological navigation so terrifying that adamantine bindings really must be cinched to hold everything remotely vague upon inspection to pillars of habit and tradition stable only by virtue of their familiarity — who would themselves yield to the same waxing and waning salience of the shifting context into which they're staked if not but for their deliberate maintenance in the face of decay? It's truly wild how savagely this transient mass will fight for a taste of what stability can be conscionably understood as barely more than illusory.

It's not as if it's some instance of alien incompatibility for one to convincingly protest the toil that keeps them incarnate — before, while, and/or after it's carried out. Being human and being conflicted seem to go hand in hand. Native to the experience is an inability to own one's essence; try as one may to encompass the thing outright, it's as if there's a lien upon half the spirit owed to irreducible ephemerality at a variable interest rate always just exceeding what one manages to cough up. It's why the narrative of the fall, of wraiths helpless but to linger after death, of eternal pursuit, and of soulmates, are so intuitively integral as plights of great cultural fascination.

Always peering behind the shoulder for something one must have missed — some elusive detail, available once in a place long forgotten, in a timeline whose only traces flit across the backdrop of consciousness, never frontally anomalous, and of such brevity that it would be mad to dissect as anything more than a chance emergence of interest owed to the mind's largely enigmatic processes. What to make of it when a circumstantial concrescence of disparate elements who happen to off one another reflect the adumbrations of some frustratingly remote gnosis, permeates one's headspace? The ethereal trickster who knits one's brow under the cover of ambiguity, and only permits their separation if one partakes with intent from a selection of normally pressing engagements, all uncanny in their dearth of allure — the whisper of something more valuable concealed among the folds of the curtains retracted to show them off.

In a sea of misunderstanding, with no land in sight — acting meaningfully might just happen through as much as the resolve to keep aiming for the horizon; the refusal to accept any subject as ultimately sorted, even before grand displays of its efficacy. Humility is the difference between one who settles below the deck of their reasoning and decides the ship itself shall serve as their island — and one who understands that it's a provision to keep the water out, and that to fulfill its purpose and carry its crew to shore, it's to be interpreted as an augmented extension of the flailing vulnerability even its captain would embody in its absence.

There is only one inhibitor precluding people from tapping into modes of being which would confer their exaltation, and it plants its flag of victory when one prepends the qualifier "overwhelming" to "anxiety" — and typically disguises as its only intelligent response: *apathy*. Cozy, worry-obliterating apathy prompts the most deflationary ascriptions of inertial irrelevance to the viability of confronting challenges. It is the ego's Hail Mary — feigning its own cessation in order to avoid complete catastrophe. It hijacks what critical evaluation would otherwise be useful for delineating solutions, and turns one away from the prospect of exposing their identity to the kind of pressure that might crack it. The heightened sensitivity and breakneck situational computation prior to a transformative struggle is both the common irritant permitted to divine one's incompetence, and the confirmation that one is capable of attaining what lies behind it. It makes sense that one would be blunted to stress if they already know the reaper's scythe to have disconnected their head from their shoulders — but to draw the line indicating whether that's what's as good as happened is entirely a matter of personal volition before the lights actually go out. It's not as if the sensation brought forth when orienting to some daunting task is anything more than the body equipping one with the chemical tools to take it on; to make a habit of fawning immediately as it arises is to craft a threat out of a helping hand.

19

CHAOTIC SEEDLINGS

W hat is the difference between someone who cringes so as to be on the verge of fainting at their own imaginings of gore, and one who gazes upon a chunk of their freshly lacerated flesh with an awful urge to penetrate deeper — overrun with dismay at the idea that it's really best they refrain from taking advantage of the opportunity to pry beneath their own surface in further investigation? Though the significance of the contrast between these temperaments typically surfaces as no more than that there ought to be some consideration for those who find themselves at odds with their exposure to bodily perforation — would a failure to concede that greater behavioral undercurrents should be markedly effected by what's as intimate as a population's varying attitudes toward the literal stuff of which they're composed, not be disingenuous?

It would be a crude simplification to assert hemophobia and morbid curiosity are mutually exclusive; many a gory horror fanatic shares the same nervous system with a squeamish, fainting wreck in the direct presence of real viscera. It's difficult to draw a line dividing what factors could be discarded in order to reduce the comparison to something as digestible as curiosity versus revulsion, as it's arguably because they've inverse connotations societally that they're inseparably enmeshed in relationships more nuanced than where there's a communally explicit object of interest or disgust. As far as that goes relating to the contents of the human body, however, the variable of violence could likely be pointed to to explain a substantial portion of the split.

The term "violent," used in virtually any capacity, however, will be half the time in a context where what it indicates would not otherwise be considered violent but for the presence of some associated intent — and will in the other half just as readily work to describe what's inert, like a tornado, or the consequences of gravity.

It seems then when categorically discriminating against violence in the sane exercise of some relevant interest — what's corporeally exposed must be done so in order to be of aid. After all this explication, what's evident is that those most resolute in following what fascinations will apparently in other cases (barring mostly the fictional) see one ostracized — are the medical professionals generally held to represent the pinnacle of social esteem. No one assumes that they're involved because of anything potentially macabre, but here by virtue precisely of that projected repugnance, there's the only fitting place for the insatiably curious on the biological front. What subset actually go into medicine in conscious angst that they'd not otherwise gain exposure to opportunities for ethical immersion into the world of insides, is incalculable — but being such a small funnel, it would really be no surprise if the methodological scrupulousness characterizing the field had anything to do with the fact that there's a mycelial bed of medics whose social survivability depended from a young age on their ability to divert attention from the tendencies their peers might not have appreciated as particularly savory, into inverse personas whose details would need to have been disproportionately pored over to maintain compared to those others, thus equipping them with their immaculate attention to detail.

This is an egregiously unfair assessment to have made, not because it's a sprawling, tacked together string of reasoning, but because it's that, and also tacitly disparages an edifice of such publicly leveraged enormity that even if it rings as somewhat cogent upon inspection, there's positively no room to substantiate it without committing oneself to the ward of the incurably uncouth. If one wishes to wander with an untethered spirit of inquiry, it's wise to beware the distance one travels in that manner while still protected by the sphere whose contents wouldn't incite grievous quantities of alarm if unearthed, is not likely to extend far beneath the surface of the community serving as ground zero for one's conceptual excavation. This in itself does not necessarily pose a threat unless one insists on sharing whatever it is they feel themselves to have discovered. Supposing the inclination to so much as mildly parade some as-of-yet integrated perspective before the (understandably) skeptical masses, proves insurmountable — it's advisable to fortify oneself against the possibility of becoming mercilessly sculpted into an example of how not to exist, by exactingly recapitulating what process was undergone to have arrived where one's newfound intrigues lay.

It's scarcely rare one exhibits their exotic notions anticipating a healthy degree of reciprocated excitement, only to be met with stifled dismay and an air of congratulations so excruciatingly false it's as though unequivocal condemnation were demanded by some sadistic demiurge to be conveyed in an impenetrably opaque, yet razor-thin film of applause. On the whole, there's no airtight way to argue the prioritization of personal prospects wrong as compared with adherence to whatever run-of-the-mill expectations constitute one's standard milieu — but to wager it's right is to stake what security the latter offers. To ignore that complication is to put oneself at dire risk while simultaneously bleeding the authenticity from the bet. Whoever holds the cards on the largest scale is not easily deceived into paying out bids won using counterfeit desperation. It's inadvisable to forfeit one's sanctuary unless what it lacks overlaps with an emptiness troublesome on the order of blood sacrifice; mere annoyance played up as something to be crucially antagonized for the sake of base satisfaction will readily transform into a many-toothed hydra with its heads all riotously hysteric at the supposition one might cast themselves into the trials of exile for anything less than crippling necessity.

Once upon a time, voyage beyond the confines of regular society and into Mother Nature's unpredictable bowels, or an equivalent lot of strife, served the quite indispensable purpose of initiation into adulthood. Such markers no longer exist with any semblance of constancy; behavior shunned as caustically explorative intertwines with what's respectably undertaken in an almost random configuration — whatever's left of a consensus on the matter seems to be that if one can successfully conjure food and shelter with it, it goes. There's a striking absence of structure dedicated to imparting what strength of character would prove deservedly rewarded, because the culture has grown beyond the point where it's functionally cognizant of its own intentions. On the level of a tribe, each member may trust the others' recommendations for what skills to develop and what habits to avoid, because there's a clear, determinate place therein which offers immediate feedback that the overarching prosperity of the group is nurtured consequential to its fulfillment.

In a way, it's as if humanity as a whole is being tested in an en masse rite of passage. No longer would it be dignified to require a guiding light through what incredible darkness it's unveiled during the course of its maturation; having moved so aggressively outward from its humble beginnings, its constituents are now called to trust themselves as intractably representative of the whole — for the use of some singular judgment, though hereto having been adequate, would prove far too myopic an escort for the vast multiplicity of interests it's unlocked for itself. The growing pains have manifested most acutely as a dissonance of pride. Though at present the self is stressed as what would prove most optimally focal for its exercise, to the chagrin of those generations who have eaten and breathed in what now would be commonly regarded a miasma of incessant cooperation, the looming disintegration they warn will be so heavily detrimental is an illusion produced by local aggregations of concern falling away to enable coalescence at a magnitude dwarfing what scattered tumors it'd been previously clumped in.

What are coveted as indivisible items of productive unity once grew larger and larger until the globe was socioculturally mapped in its entirety, and since then have been dissolving back into smaller units as Earth's physical limits have across the board been subconsciously confirmed as homo sapiens' principal sandbox — the need to actually unify under something like a single government inconsequentially skipped, since there's drastically less energy spent investing in oneself as an internationally acceptable entity than there is trying to weld countries together at their geriatric political strata. The fear of oligarchic hegemony saturating discourse among traditionalists is an empty, arrogant terror predicated on a lack of faith that their entire age demographic across the planet will, on account of nothing more than time, be gradually replaced with an attitude taking it as granted that a person's hope for themselves undoubtedly mirrors, not in specifics, but as a property of being alive, an interminably respectable quality in every other human being.

Maybe it's wishful thinking to project such credibility onto the human enterprise — painting elders as inveterate neurotics and sentencing them to the sea of forgetfulness on account of their worries might be no different than the very anxiety-stricken promises of divine retribution they lord over everyone else in attempts to forcibly append a stable sort of future onto whatever it is that's going on.

Across cases though, the common underlying principle which when routed appears to invoke colossal discord, is a kind of personal faith which demands nothing of anyone else. To foist imaginary obligations onto others, venting what doubt would otherwise pollute one's determination in the method they abide to attain mastery over their situation, is an offer to forsake the learning process in exchange for the sweet, empty sustenance of external validation. One gives their power away to those who never ask for it; it is not only folly to pawn off what's worth anything solely to oneself, but the effort to make an appraisal exacerbates the descent of its value — for the integrity of an instrument the wielder of which seeks in panic to abandon is nearly certainly dilapidated. Just because in theory its greatest manifestation might call unsolicited attention — to use that promise as a way of cashing out on what will never develop to such heights without the care of its requisite custodian, is tragically foolish. It is to voluntarily front one's children, bartering for a bit of gold.

20

MOMENTUM

To start from scratch, or to build upon what came before? Before it's known what depths one's plundered coming to their current place in space and time, it doesn't just seem feasible, but wise to advantageously exploit what one tucked for themselves in troves once glistening with the promise it could lighten the load pending the descent of some ungovernable tribulation. Only come the day one finds themselves prompted long after its entombment to unearth the contents of pride once cherished — will they find themselves gargantuan, and what lies before them but a meager offering. Though cursed might it seem being not able to rely on the spoils of past triumphs — it's a rare blessing to find oneself pinned without the resources they'd planned to have at their disposal, not because the path they trod had been strayed from, but because they've come so far that they deceive themselves into dependence on skills that they still hold in high regard from long ago, and had stowed away for the future, to the effect of a child gifting a good luck charm to one entering the front lines of war.

Bittersweet nostalgia and the realization what dragons one has to face can and will be conquered not by anything defensively hoarded — but by prowess cultivated having sprung forth from fields of poison mist and from weaving foothills dotted with beasts and from serpentine routes carved up bluffs through crashing waves and wind and rain, and amusingly enough on account of the stock one placed in some merit rendered meek after all of what its inspiration served to overcome, came to pass. One finds themselves, always, at square one — and with much ground to cover. The binary quandary, to lean into what's ahead, or to shy away from it, and surely sometimes insanity is the only explanation for one who'd decide to proceed, and that just goes to show even though the struggle is elementary in its organization — that that does not make its tests less burdensome.

What else could be expected? It's inane to think any prolonged absence of tension resides on the horizon, and yet so too to think the trek forth worth nothing in light of that. There's always the door out, but suicide is perhaps the most revolting infraction, the most egregious insult to the ever-looming boon of what could be. Even though it would take little more than the deductive prowess of a drooling ignoramus to confidently declare that the thing is rigged, and that any trophy at any end could be shown illusory with nothing more than an extrapolation of the fact that a cycle resets such that what follows its conclusion is undeniably identical in its arrangement to what preceded it, with hardly more than an alteration of details adequately trivial to be classified as cosmetic — there's something sacred enough about playing the game that that disparagement, justified as it may seem, correctly if inexplicably registers as a plastic revelation to most.

It's as though there's a minimum quantity of movement across this plane absolutely prerequisite to the appreciation of the dance — even though it would seem rational to ascertain the pros and cons of what's going on from where one stands, from where one rots if static, from where one is pushed and pressured by unseen forces to take part in the spectacle of being. The leading hand is offered, and yet just as often it's met with hesitation, furious curiosity, tantrums thrown pleading for clarification as though from there that would or could grace eyes designed to peruse the show as a participant in lieu of a bystander.

Nothing in this place is rooted to anything not itself in flux — even the ground of the planet, that great foundation commanding the most stability, soars unameliorably through the void. How is there such demand for the abolition of psychological vertigo when there's nothing evaluably ample to act as a base upon which dizziness could transpire? The apparition of security must itself be what causes the destruction of balance — only those dependent on a foothold would see fit to declare its loss a hazard to safety. Each is thrust into chaos on parturition; insisting anything one involves themselves with thereafter might somehow loose itself from the underlying possibility of total upheaval is maniacal.

Momentum is essential for sustained equilibrium. In all things, it's easier to hold steady with some amount of action for leverage than it is to gather oneself from a standstill — this is why one's engagements first thing in the morning will tend to color the entirety of their ensuing day. One lies awash with the passage of time during each long sleep — rising thereafter obliged to shoulder its full brunt from peak inertia. Mastering a clean shift from the comfort of unconsciousness to the sudden awareness that time hadn't for the whole restful duration been courteous enough to so much as glance back or hesitate in its dogged advance, and will coldly permit one their idleness for as long as they opt to postpone their forthright launch into its current — is the kind of task which though readily yielding to a blind, forceful transition from horizontal on the bed to vertical on the floor, is completely inscrutable insofar as one might seek to establish some kind of impermeable doctrine which through uninvested observation alone might manufacture the motivation necessary to transcend the tranquilizing properties of silken coziness.

Any contrivable series of thoughts applied to this end off the cuff on a given morning are likely to fall prey to the amorphous litany of anxious ideas fruitlessly revolving in bids to generate forward motion from nothing. This is taken for granted here, because if there *were* a singular, deliberately elected concept competent to function as a propellant — it would arise like a tsunami, forcing one past the threshold of wakefulness as the solitary object of mind, and by that virtue never need to be summoned to the secondary end of getting oneself up. This generally seems to be the character of what internal emergences end up responsible for purging the accumulated dross owed to one's matutinal bouts of senseless pondering, and prompting the legitimate start of the day — though in jarring contrast to what would be an ideal means, as it lacks the autonomously pioneered quality of a fully unforced solution. To seamlessly stack one's intentions from the instant they begin to germinate favorably in the subtle guise of thought, through the incrementally concretized medium of utterance, and into the matured expression of action, with no contradictions from any one stage in that evolution to another — this is what it means to master oneself. It's an affair of condensation.

It seems for this to be carried out effectively, and on a consistent basis, there needs to be some preliminary assemblage of behavior both unstained by sin (meaning to miss the mark, i.e., free from what one could conscionably call for themselves any critically undermining idiocies — identifiable as those deeds whose malignance is sufficient to turn one against themselves in hostility, whatever they may be), and temporally sizable such that it carries enough power through evening to fracture the hazy passivity of the dawn in which it culminates. One is welcome to spin aimlessly at the mercy of what confounding suppositional eddies they muster trying to delineate what's sensible a priori — but this is quite like trying to confront a fear of flight stood safely on the ground, and accomplishes little to the end of successfully engaging in a mentionable journey. It's as insane to rely on oneself in stasis for gainfully blossoming information as it is to interrogate an unaffiliated suspect, command a brand new infant to negotiate the complexity of walking the moment they arrive on the scene, or wring out a dry washcloth.

Vying for purchase from the supposed sanctuary of paralysis is like analyzing the lore of an MMORPG in the midst of a raid. It's a personal decision to allow anyone else's historical predilections mental space in spite of one's carnal impermanence — but for the record, that latter tragedy is as good of an excuse to double down on a course of action as one can bet they'll get their hands on while they're here. The simplicity with which a given path may be followed can have an understandably unsettling impression — wherever one sticks their flag, and whatever color it is, it will irreversibly carve its way through the annals one occupies in their time. Refusing to relinquish the habit of juggling one's allegiances for fear that otherwise what harmlessly glancing accusations shouldered in the brief intervals they hold any, might eventually attain some potency — can be tempting; this is the terror of growing up. The trade-off in question is between innocent ineffectuality and directional adeptness. Everyone starts life holding a can of spray paint with the cap stuck on go — whether it's pointed at a substrate sturdy enough to host anything potentially interesting is entirely a matter of individual discretion.

For the contents of one's world to be interesting, that being a trait manifesting on the brink of incomprehensibility — suggests a kind of intellectual chase is at hand, and by extension an unbridled course outward from one's centermost haven of cerebral stagnance. What's ascertained to be lacking from a place chocked full with the muck of ceaselessly recycled dread and memory, only appears so the same way a Thanksgiving dinner would to one having stuffed themselves in advance with tasteless gruel. It's impossible to manage more than feigned appreciation for fascinations one has no space for; one must breach a certain emptiness in the skies of the mind wherefrom the immensity of daily pressures may be looked upon as trifling — if they ache to be stolen from the dense torpor of their own inhibitive condescension.

Isolation is perhaps the worst enemy of the unwittingly guarded, for there's a solid chance what bindings they fret to part with are those forged to secure against the anticipated infiltration of another, previous set, and so on — layers of armor indefinitely donned but for the relief of trusted companions' tolerated prodding to crack them occasionally. Once one is allowed to eject their own interpretation of risk from the standard inventory of tools for moving through the thick of Earth's troubles, the marvel of living rapidly devolves into an insufferable labor. Notice though, the notion of risk not only dissipates in its legitimacy if an overabundance of shelter taints one's environment — but so too if one fancies themselves subject to peril substantial enough that it dwarfs the probability of its evasion, as this passively works to validate a compulsive pattern of depressively folding in the face of opportunity.

That latter event might not instinctually present as a formidable barrier, as it would be easy to falsify the logic by pitting one's refusal to swallow a handful of sleeping pills against the inevitability of their demise, thereby instantly spotlighting their hypocrisy — but an approach in this vein will generally be reprehended as excessively abrasive, and then to boot, everyone still alive can be accused to some degree of subservience to circumstance. This does not mean it isn't disproportionately overused as a safety mechanism and/or linchpin for complaint — only that it's ubiquitous as those things because with the requisite nuance, one is able to wield the art of the guilt-trip so that it cuts precisely between the accuser's limit of risk-tolerance, and *their* continued existence. That pocket is the last bastion of the chronically horrified, from which few if any outside can provide release if taken up. It's constructed to weaponize incoming encouragement, and relies on its projected injuriousness to perpetuate seclusion; assertive support is spun as senselessly aggravated, and gentle assurance, as damagingly ignorant.

21

DEATH

In the twilight hours of life, though rife with evidence of degradation and loss, where it seems from outside that the gleam in an elder's eyes should come only from what youth around them they've to dwell on and vicariously revel in — the black door through which they're soon ushered spoils none of its contents before crossed, and stands therefore a greater adventure than positively everything preceding it. It is the most absolute conceivable boundary. One would think, death sharing a level of secrecy trumping the most untouched reaches of nature and the highest tiers of society both by several orders of magnitude — that there might generally be a more pronounced sense of urgency respecting the disclosure of what's in wait behind it.

One could chalk it up to the perceived difficulty with which such a revelation might be accomplished, and subsequently reason there's hardly anything worth a preemptive probe since everyone eventually gets tossed off the edge of incarnation anyhow — but that hardly follows as a satisfying explanation for the lack of excitement. For as mysterious as it is, the associated reaction to its mention never quite seems to be an expression of genuine, giddy impatience — at least not publicly. The dead, apparently, comprise too secret a society to really appreciate.

The central quandary gazing into any lifeless visage is the following: Though clearly something primary to the animation of the mass of flesh lying before one, is *gone* — is it reasonable to say it's *gone somewhere?* As for sleep, what's probably death's nearest physical parallel, it's proper to say one "goes to sleep" the same way in which one goes to the market — but conveyance to a literal destination is hardly implied that same way. There's also the unique complication that both sleep and death are fundamental to the process of life — but in perfectly opposite senses. Sleep plays the role of a charging apparatus, without which carnal deterioration swiftly ensues. Death is its waking counterpart — paramount to the acquisition of corporeal fuel. The former revitalizes via internal mechanisms; the latter conducts its invigoration as an emissary of extrinsic sacrifice.

Death arguably defines life, at least for creatures with the intelligence to recognize it haunts every horizon, facilitating the comprehension of existence as a subcategory rather than some cognitively inviolable firmament forcing one's highest fears and appreciations alike to fall merely among its contents, which compared to the grandiosity of life as both infinite and finite simultaneously, space-time both boundless yet scheduled for cessation at the edge of the fabled scythe — captivate about as efficaciously as sandbox toys. It allows one to hold, in the form of a conceptual article, the phenomenon of being as such. There is no question that this capacity comes at enormous cost, as humans are the only creatures obliged to confront the grand finale face-up on the cosmic chopping block — every tedious moment exercising the benefits of (relatively) higher consciousness manditorily obstructed lest inordinate quantities of connective cogitation overtake what's conducively loosed in the confines of the civil participation one depends on to maintain some semblance of a reliably equilibrated material circumstance.

The ignorance of an animal and the ignorance of a human are two vastly different beasts. Where an animal flies blind in service to its aims, a human is constantly vulnerable to the criticism that behaving likewise is principally to their detriment — and yet each passing moment mints ten-thousand novel points of consideration, all the decades of one's life like the ceaseless climb up to an ever-ascending peak. The human imposition of dimensions superfluous to an earnest quest for an elixir which would somehow bring them apotheosis amid the merciless thrashing of waxing and waning and waxing and waning and waxing and waning... fashion, gastronomy, entertainment; much more than warranting pride as proof that culture is high and humanity's conquest birthed jubilant frivolity — is a desperate, faulty, mimetic plea of intellectuality for the animal respite forbidden it.

The task of justifiably swallowing oxygen is like using a bent stick to realize an alien blueprint, *and yet it must be done*. There's the limit, then, right there — the animal respite in question: that it must be done. It isn't as easily teased as from a salamander's shady frond or the albatross' cozy currents of air — but the certainty that one must proceed with their confounding lot is exactly the kind of inarguable conviction upon which one's scattered collection of concerns may be gently laid for patient sorting; one must go *through* life, not because of some lofty imperative, but because that's definitionally the scenario given a step in any direction taken from the inside of something. The incitement of insanity by virtue of calculable time's behemothic immensity, is subtly remedied by one's very willingness to consider it a problem; the weight of reflecting on the past and projecting oneself into the future is balanced adequately by nothing more than the license to take heart and communally savor in living through a battle of such spiritual magnitude that even at rest the prospect of total bodily termination seems a not completely unreasonable alternative to facing it.

Take all it consumes as evidence; the void envies the means to reflect light and produce sound and make a mess of things. Laugh into it — the deepest reaches of its bowels are choiceless but to echo, and few creatures are gifted the opportunity to relish in awareness they stand inches from its mandibles. No brighter light can emanate but from that which elects to shine against a backdrop of inescapable darkness; eternity ought to shudder that the inhabitants of an inconsequential speck in the boondocks of one of two trillion galaxies would in unambiguous sobriety choose to dance despite the knowledge of its omnipotent maw. Celestial retaliation is simple, and ineffably gratifying — the existentially preposterous not only implodes if it sets on an attitude of open acceptance, but will act as a thrall for those who'd champion its beauty.

Doubt is not a venom, but a poison; it'll only corrode if voluntarily imbibed. There's a game goes on where people use that fact to transform the instance of death into a fulcrum functioning to relate the lengths that straddle it to one another in a custom configuration. Death is like an epistemological free space of the bingo variety — pointless to leave unattended when under pressure it will anyway effortlessly fill itself using a conglomeration assembled with one's best approximations of what's sensible granted its presence. The point is something like agnostic purism respecting death is hollow since death's approach will distill any otherwise amorphous suppositions of it into a mythos at least sufficiently substantial to act in accordance with. I.e. — even assuming one finds nothing satisfactorily verifiable about what transpires after the end from outside a foxhole, the yawning grave like a camera shutter reduces extraneous information until a crystal clear picture predicated completely on its impending closure emerges in consequence, and so there's faith influentially involved whether one likes it or not, and as a result, the refusal to outright commit to a biased assessment of death, perhaps counterintuitively, is closer to indefensible philosophical procrastination than exemplary adherence to testable claims. It's baseless to wager codifying assertions about what underpins behavior are somehow communicatively superior to behaviors themselves — unmodified reactions amount to a much more dependable medium from which to sculpt penetrating structures of reasoning than do prefabricated viewpoints, which are liable to falter grievously in their integrity as the subjects of their application stray so much as remotely from the Platonic ideal of demonstrably relevant context. Ultimately undiscardable — the quality of one's faith should be autonomously investigated, not inherited from some external edifice as if what without dedicated attention would remain shrouded in mystery until minutes prior to one's demise could be conferred offhand by another person.

Debatability aside — the interesting thing about deliberately manipulating one's impressions of a bottomlessly potentiated point of significance, in addition to the mechanics of it, is the extent of its effect in validating particular sets of choices. In principle, the scene one abides as painted postmortem will effect one's movement toward it in a manner consistent with what would constitute its optimal encounter — just the same way one's strongest intimations of an anticipated date's preferences will automatically prompt any important preparatory adjustments. The depth of this effect, though unguarded against repudiation from the angle that since death withholds its secrets seamlessly it's damnable and unwarranted, is reflective of, and must reflect at least in proportion to some minimum ante paid upon birth in light of what responses death evokes from all — a correspondingly entrenched belief. That is to say there's a swath of spiritual leverage beholden to every person whose consequential range begins above nonexistent. Very well — and where does that range top out? The answer to this question reveals that in stark contrast to inane — faith in something specific as the true shape of the unfathomable is accurately characterized as a similarly indefinite wellspring of power. To convince oneself of anything about death is to unlock, as in the swinging of a golf club, the faculty of follow-through — but pertaining to the scale of an entire lifetime.

Skepticism surrounding superficially similar proponents seems to source the lot of it directed at those dispositionally gnostic with regards to death, most notably due to an insistence on appraising statements based on the illusory grounds of *what they are in and of themselves*, as differentiated from their value *in effect*. This impasse typically won't emerge where language has been widely and uniformly mapped onto the matrices of things people have, will, and do experience — because those subsets of stimuli formulate a network of static, communally referenceable objects whose mutual recognizability is in the wider interests of the communities wherein they're found. The fluidity of basic ontological discernment is a ubiquitously desirable effect of most of what will ever be verbally addressed; everyone has the freedom to persistently refer to toilets as refrigerators, and that doesn't happen because it would juxtapose contexts in a way quite understandably striking most as an annoyance.

With this in place, however, there spawns an unbelievably deceptive pitfall where individuals become unable to digest the notion that a statement constructed using familiar words from their mother tongue could or would be anything other than mistaken, in jest, or some sort of demonic bastardization of meaning and language — if an effort to comprehensively track its denotation on the whole leads one into unrecognizable territory. This is precisely what happens between people who "disagree" about the implications of death. Contention about what happens after death finds all parties extremely gratuitous insofar as their implication what's posited among them could reside in the same system of conceptual identifiability — what's addressed being impervious both to retrospective *and* active analysis. Just because a statement lacks a delineably common undercurrent does not mean it's barren of utility for the one who utters it, and a personalized conception of worldly departure, in addition to being a most formidably elusive target to force into a standardized linguistic package — is tremendously alluring in its offer to immediately catalyze lasting change if only one would opt to evict whatever occupies the psychological real estate it would necessarily replace.

One might stumble into confusion analyzing belief as a discovery versus as a skill. Is it that it grows and strengthens in response to diligent affirmation — or that what dormant potential it holds is unveiled because of excess which must be scraped away? There's a tricky bit of an impasse here which on the surface might appear exempt from resolution — but in fact what's gained through each perspective successfully accounts for the other's blind spot. In order to simplify the evaluation, the terms employed henceforth will pose it as a contest between talent and hard work, where the former stands in place of belief as discovery, and the latter in place of belief as skill — thus preserving the vital divergence such that the original question will in the end be attended concurrently with the equally pressing, and likely more familiar, age-old debate.

The usual understanding of talent is as a natural aptitude or skill. Hard work is something like the self-imposed, enduring effort toward obtaining a skill. There is nothing, then, contradictory about the idea that the aptitude for hard work might be entirely of the same prodigal ancestry as anything else one appears to, without interference, excel in. If one imagines, as well, that an organically gifted pianist ages to forty without having so much as laid eyes on a piano, the talent at issue can never germinate until some introduction to the instrument is undergone, which, one's initial contact with any discipline being as a rule the most difficult — insinuates no dearth of preparatory work for them to uncover their proficiency in it. In effect, the amount of consistent effort required to milk any supposed talent, is, for all intents and purposes — equivalent to the amount of talent not outrageously declared possessed by a hard worker with comparable results. Really this discussion is little more than splitting hairs over the difference between a sculptor and a painter; when the cards are down, addition versus subtraction do not as systems of creation intrinsically trump one another — lauding talent or hard work to the exclusion of the other is unproductive. In the domain of belief, the difference manifests as that between someone who is born and bred Roman Catholic, versus one who takes up faith down the road with no unconscious presupposition that their position is singular in its infallible arbitration of truth. In effect, this will deeply impact the greater cultural environments in which one finds themselves — information unwisely neglected unless the related belief is strong enough to foster spirituality independent of the established local resources for doing so.

Beyond all embellishments, faith on its own is virtually impossible to speak about without coming across as *fixated on the immaterial*, which as a string of words without context is jarringly oxymoronic enough; appearing rational to a mind invested in a higher power, the opposite to a mind preoccupied with the physical, rational again to one in tune with the fact that any physical thing can be endlessly dissected in search of underlying solidity to no avail, opposite again to one taking "immaterial" to simply mean that category of things it's senseless to concentrate on, rational again to one who knows full well the only way to concentrate on the immaterial is to be devoid of sense, and that that's the most enjoyable preoccupation there is, opposite again to one who'd shun fixation in all its forms, and so on and so forth. More than anything, this ridiculous dance represents the majority of interaction between the spiritual factions, and within them. It ought to be forgiven a thousand times over for one to think the lot of them approximately glorified asylums.

Eventually at some point deep into all this weaving madness, when finally for the last time there's been a twist of the plot, instead of being run ragged another increment by the labor of securing clarification, the absurdity of the whole thing collapses under its own weight, and the message, served on a bed of cosmic hilarity, sat pristine atop the rubble — is that *there was never anything to worry about in the first place*. It's an answer from nowhere, grace without expectation, gain the type to savor after having had nothing to lose. Then slowly, gently, it fades once more into the background from whence it came, leaving nothing but a whisper and a wink inside a memory, like a glimmer of magic tucked inside a pocket that will never need to be opened — not more than the intimation of its presence sufficient to set one at ease.

The strength to spread one's arms, close one's eyes, smile, and tip backwards into what could be forever, is priceless — and in a way, it's the source of addiction. Reprieve, whether from fatigue itself, an ungovernable mass of stimulation, boredom, etc. — is readily available in the chemical confines of matter. Though everyone loves their pets, this conundrum is equivalent to the reluctant subservience a wild creature demonstrates as it becomes irreparably domesticated. That is to say, if one lacks the gall to independently pursue what lies beyond the shackles of the mundane for fear of lunacy, or bodily harm, or judgement, the tragedy is not that the world is a mess or that things make no sense or that the situation is depressing and institutionally schizophrenic beyond redemption, but that the morsels of respite scattered between otherwise great fields of disdainful entrapment are tacitly admitted more enticing than that situation's inversion — that the terror of liberation is greater than that of imprisonment.

ACKNOWLEDGMENTS

My deepest gratitude to my mother, who is an unrivaled beacon of positivity and inspiration, impossible to dishearten for longer than a moment — and who scarcely knows a fraction of her caliber as a parent. Endless thanks to Sarah, whose love for family and invincible perseverance consistently overcome trials the likes of which have irremediably crippled countless spirits of lesser conviction. To Juliann, whose tireless drive and boundless vision serve as examples for all men, young and old alike — and whose brotherhood surpasses the most precious stones in value. To Terry — for the delicious food, and for sharing sunny Arizona afternoons gazing over her lakes, engaged in spectacularly lucid contemplation.

And thank you, reader, for without you this work is little more than a lifeless mass of condensed pulp. If you enjoyed it, and have the time to spare — I humbly invite you to leave a review.

https://mitchpo.co